Loss of Empire

LOSS OF EMPIRE

Legal Lynching, Vigilantism, and African American Intellectualism in the 21st Century

L.V. Gaither

Africa World Press, Inc.

P.O. Box 1892
Trenton, NJ 08607

P.O. Box 48
Asmara, ERITREA

Africa World Press, Inc.

P.O. Box 1892
Trenton, NJ 08607

P.O. Box 48
Asmara, ERITREA

Book design: Saverance Publishing Services
Cover design: Dapo Ojo-Ade

Photos, left to right: Portrait of abolitionist Frederick Douglass (1817-1895), photographed by Matthew Brady (1823-1896) in 1890 (Image Source: Library of Congress. Permission: public domain). Walls Unit Penitentiary, Huntsville, Texas, the building where the state of Texas administers executions by lethal injection. Courtesy of L.V. Gaither, Houston, Texas. Portrait of Booker T. Washington, photographed by Frances Benjamin Johnston (1864-1952) in 1902 (Image Source: Library of Congress. Permission: public domain). The background photo is an enlarged and cropped image of Fred Gildersleeve's photo of the lynching of Jesse Washington in 1916 (Image Source: Library of Congress: Permission: public domain).

Library of Congress Cataloging-in-Publication Data

Gaither, L. V.
Loss of empire: legal lynching, vigilantism, and African American intellectualism in the 21st century / L.V. Gaither.
   p. cm.
Includes bibliographical references and index.
ISBN 1-59221-431-2 (cloth) -- ISBN 1-59221-432-0 (pbk.)
   1. Lynching--United States. 2. Vigilantes--United States. 3. African Americans--Crimes against. 4. Gildersleeve, Fred A., 1881-1958. 5. Abu-Jamal, Mumia. 6. Byrd, James, d. 1998. 7. African Americans--Intellectual life--21st century. 8. African American leadership. 9. African Americans--Civil rights. 10. United States--Race relations. I. Title.

HV6457.G35 2006
364.1'34--dc22

                        2006014712

Wealth maketh many friends, but the poor is separated from his neighbor.

-Proverbs 19:4

For we wrestle not against flesh and blood, but against principalities, against powers, against the rulers of the darkness of this world, against spiritual wickedness in high places.

-Ephesians 6:12

Table of Contents

Preface

The pervasive chaos engulfing the lives of millions throughout the world has its origins within the core of American empire. In our name, empire's last resort to global dominance—its military and prison industrial complexes—have been unleashed to prey on those peripheral nations who resist the social and cultural limitations of capitalism. The endless expropriation of the wealth of other nations is a dangerous trend that has accompanied the ascension of global capitalism all along, but such military excesses have finally created an asymmetrical conflict in which continued and chaotic uncertainties are sure to follow in its wake.

Only massive political change will alter the course of empire's decline, and this would be a good thing, for the loss of empire provides humanity with the opportunity to do what the Caribbean revolutionary Frantz Fanon urged us to do just a mere four decades ago: Turn over a new leaf, work out new concepts, and set afoot a new man. Yet there is no agenda or plan of political action from the American Left to provide a true alternative to the white global social order. And because of a lack of social consciousness on the part of leaders, most of us can only pray that God will have mercy on our seemingly helpless souls.

According to the Bureau of Justice statistics, if the current rates of imprisonment continue as they are, 32 percent of African American males will enter state or federal prison during their lifetime. But such a staggering projection sheds little light on the issue of black male imprisonment. There are other consequences. For instance, nearly one out of ten African American children has parents who are incarcerated in either state or federal prisons,

and many of those projected to be incarcerated are themselves
children. Education has always been important, but there are
more African American men being imprisoned than graduating
from high school.

It is one thing to not be able to catch a cab in New York City
(a common complaint issued by black professional intellectuals
and/or celebrities when being interviewed on television by white
journalists); it is quite another to come of age under a system
of anti-black discipline and punishment, new forms of political
surveillances, racial and ethnic repression, and massive imprisonment; to be targeted by the color of your skin or the geographical
location you've been confined to because of your racial and class
origin—as an increasing majority of African American youth can
attest to. The effect of the massive imprisonment on families and
communities has brought about communities in chaos.

In 2002, African American women accounted for more than
70 percent of the HIV/AIDS cases in women. Again, such a
startling statistic sheds little light on the negative impact HIV/
AIDS is having within African American communities. African
American children with AIDS represent more than 65 percent of
the pediatric cases, and African American teenagers aged 13-19,
according to a report issued by the Kaiser Institute, accounted
for 61 percent of the reported HIV/AIDS cases in 2001. Meanwhile, no alarm bells have been sounded. Even the vice president
of the United States, in one of the staged presidential debates,
expressed his unawareness of such a crisis.

For the past two presidential elections, African American
intellectuals have stood by idly as both corporate-controlled
parties have effectively Jim Crowed a significant segment of the
African American population out of the electoral arena, but the
consecutive victories of Bush and Cheney shed little light on how
increasingly marginalized African Americans have become in
the public sphere. In truth, throughout American empire black
political mobility has been contradicted by a resurgent ideology
of whiteness, and African American intellectuals appear to be

less willing than incapable of properly responding. This book is an attempt to introduce some of the ideas I have accumulated over the past ten years regarding African American intellectual fashions and responses to what the late W.E.B. Dubois referred to as the color line.

Turning South Again: Re-Thinking Modernism/Re-Reading Booker T. by Houston A. Baker, Jr.[1] informs my approach to writing the first chapter, "Rethinking Fred Gildersleeve's Lynching Photography in the Age of Legal Lynching." Baker's analysis of black modernism, unimpeded by narrow disciplinary strictures, made clear the pervasive centrality of confederate hegemony in empire's geopolitical trajectory. Despite the pains taken by many of the most popular scholars in the United States to subvert the specter of race in contemporary discourse, no less than the majority of African Americans live in imprisoned-like conditions. Such conditions cannot be separated from the black modernist project of the early twentieth century, which was forestalled by the South's antiblack policing, lynching, and prison apparatus. The hallmark of this epochal moment in the expansion of white supremacy was the state's expropriation of vigilante methods of repression to subdue black progress.

Chapter Two, "All James T. Byrd, Jr. Wanted Was a Ride: Lynching and Policing Powers in Texas," was originally published in Joy James's *States of Confinement: Policing, Detentions, and Prisons*[2] as "All The Brother Wanted Was A Ride." Other than the title, there are no significant changes. It reexamines leadership responses to antiblack policing and vigilantism. In my view, antiblack violence needs to be synthesized into its totality; only then will the political structures that perpetuate it be clearly revealed.

There were several critical responses from reviewers of the third chapter, "African American Leadership Responses to the Increasing Significance of Whiteness," some of which should be acknowledged here. The most noticeable was that I overstated the issue regarding the historical responses to black nationalism from what I loosely referred to as the Left. I characterize the historical relationship as fiercely and endlessly antagonistic. In fact, I did not put too much emphasis on any particular example, nor was I too critical of any particular individual, which was another criticism of the essay.

For one, I am at the present mostly concerned about African American leadership responses to whiteness, and how such reactionary and cautious responses have infiltrated post-civil rights political discourse. My conclusion at the present historical moment is that the abolition of whiteness, if left to Europeans themselves, will remain a permanent feature of the global political and economic order known as capitalism, or whatever order comes after. No significant political action can take shape under such conditions. Others would disagree, however.

One reviewer suggested that unlike Nation of Islam leader minister Louis Farrakhan who is a national leader, Manning Marable, Cornel West, and William Julius Wilson should not be criticized because they are simply cultural critics. In addition, the reviewer felt I had capitulated to any and all forms of nationalism. However, I have always been perplexed by how easily African American nationalist leaders of the past like Marcus Garvey, Honorable Elijah Muhummad, and Malcolm X, or those of the present like Louis Farrakhan, Molefi Asante, and the late Kwame Ture (Stokely Carmichael) fall sway to groundless criticisms issued by establishment commentators but, when such criticisms elicit responses, how taken aback these people become. In my view, academicians, particularly those who take it upon themselves to jump into the political fray, need to be held accountable as much as those who, for good or bad, are undeniably legitimate political leaders.

There was also an assumption that I relied on Harold Cruse's pendulum theory, which put forth the argument that since the 1800s African American leadership has been split along integrationist and nationalist lines. Cruse's widely known book, *The Crisis of the Negro Intellectual*, however, isn't referenced in any of the four essays and wasn't taken into account in my analysis, although in hindsight it should perhaps be made known that I generally agree with him on what seems to me such an obvious point.[3]

Based on my experiences and study of history, I felt that a critical sketch of contemporary African American leadership responses to whiteness should begin with Frederick Douglass's career as an abolitionist struggling against the enslavement of Africans in the new world. Written accounts of his life and politics provide the earliest narrative of an African American activist working within the confines of the liberal project and clearly illuminate the frustration and limitation of working within interracial political formations in America.

The reason we study a people's history is to inform us in our quest to make clearer sense of the present. For me, a study of Douglass's life is most useful when placed within the context of the unfinished African American struggle for liberation. As C.L.R. James once noted, "after all the work the Negro historians have done on him, his significance, both as an American and as an American Negro, eludes them."[4] This might be generally true but wasn't so with regard to William S. McFeely's biography, *Frederick Douglass*, to which I am indebted.[5]

Perhaps the present moment in history is the first where African American leadership appears incognito. I agree with Robert C. Smith's conclusion in his book, *We Have No Leaders: African Americans in the Post-Civil Rights Era* (1996):

> Three consequences flow from the post-civil rights era leadership's inability to act. First, in spite of—indeed in a sense because of—a bewildering variety of organized groups, old and new, the black community today remains largely unorganized. Second, blacks remain dependent on a decaying party (and party system) that attempts to maintain itself in power by ignoring black policy interests and symbolically distancing itself from black people altogether, although blacks provide the party a fifth of its national vote. Third, as a result in part of a lack of effective organization and dependency on the Democratic Party,

> blacks have been unable to develop the requisite pressures
> to get the system to respond to its most pressing post-
> civil rights era demand: the need for employment in the
> context of some kind of overall program of internal ghetto
> reconstruction and development. The result is a core
> black community, euphemistically referred to as the inner
> city, that is increasingly poor, dispossessed and alienated.
> Meanwhile the leaders of white America respond with
> neglect, contemptuously suggesting that unless there is a
> change in the "values" of African Americans, nothing can
> be done about the deterioration of their communities.[6]

Smith's summation of what could only be seen as a crisis in leadership also points to another criticism of this work: that there
is no call for an alternative political party. It seems—to some
at least—that my analysis obligated me to put forth the idea of
an alternative political party. As I see it, far too much emphasis
has been placed on electoral politics and not enough on political issues most immediately impacting African American life.
However, if a political party will prove instrumental in helping us
navigate through the present chaotic crisis, then there is definitely
a need for an alternative party. As the 2004 presidential election
confirmed, the Democratic Party has been the graveyard of all
social movements of the twentieth and twenty-first centuries.

Chapter four, "Black Movements Toward Freedom: Mumia
Abu-Jamal and Empire's Prisoners of War," is a revision of the
previously published "Conviction Or A Fine?: Are There Political Prisoners and POWs In The Good Ole U.S. of A?," which
appeared in S.E. Anderson and Tony Medina's *In Defense of
Mumia*.[7] At the time, the movement to free political prisoners
and prisoners of war was beginning to grow, and Mumia's case
was a large reason for this. Although many more of us know the
answer today, the question whether there were political prisoners
and prisoners of war within empire's borders was still in the air
prior to September 11, 2001. This essay was an attempt to rec-
oncile my views and political activities against the death penalty,
racial profiling, and the massive growth of the prison industrial

complex with the work that needed to be done around POWs and political prisoners. I viewed Mumia Abu-Jamal's case as representative of the U.S. government's attempt to criminalize black people, from its introduction of slave codes, to COINTELPRO, to today's racial profiling apparatus. In 2002, I lectured at several universities on the topic of prisons and the death penalty, and, thus, it was necessary for me to construct a political and historical context for the present growth of prisons. Although the delineations I have drawn between the American Revolution, civil war, and civil rights movements are not put forth as conclusive, they allow us a much clearer picture of the political role of prisons relative to African American communities of resistance.

Chapter One

Rethinking Fred Gildersleeve's Lynching Photography in the Age of Legalized Lynching

> A lynching right now, when the attention of the nation is focused on Arkansas as a result of the flood situation, would cause irreparable harm to the reputation of the state. I beseech you to leave the matter to the courts.
>
> –Rev. J. O. Johnson

Jesse Washington's unclothed body is saturated in coal oil and lies prostrate on what seems to be a dry-goods box that has been set aflame by two men standing over his body. As Washington's helpless body is being burned (he is probably still alive in the photo), one of the men has managed to cast the chain tied to Washington's neck over a steady tree limb, enabling the body to be easily hoisted high enough for the entire audience to clearly witness.

The townspeople are "dressed to kill"—they are wearing their Sunday clothes. The men, half of whom have on neckties, wear white brimmed hats. This was hardly a spur-of-the-moment event. It appears to be well-planned, at least premeditated, and although many of the people are smiling, laughing, and appear to be in high spirits, it cannot be determined from looking at the photo whether they are behaving in a rowdy fashion. They have surrounded the body, but there is a clearly defined space between them and the victim Washington. As spectators, they are not emotionally beside themselves. With the exception of the men ushering in the spectacle, the crowd's collective gaze is fixated on the victim's body. Included among them are three very noticeable black people—two men and one woman—standing near the periphery of the crowd.[1]

I am not surprised to see them; I was expecting them, a point I'll return to. But when I pointed them out to the curator of an exhibit featuring the collection of photos compiled by James Allen and published in his book *Without Sanctuary*, he concluded that I had mistaken them for being black. "They were simply positioned in a manner where the sun's reflection made them appear to be nonwhite," he said. Another time, I was delivering a lecture to a group of black college students in upstate New York and included Fred A. Gildersleeve's photo of Jesse Washington's lynching to illustrate a point as well as engage questions from the audience—I anticipated not having the answer to most, as I was still grappling for answers.

A couple weeks earlier, the same photo was used in a lecture I gave to a group comprised of mostly nonblack students, and there was a loud collective gasp from them in response to their recognition of these individuals. But among the black students there was an unmoving silence. I later asked a comrade who attended the New York lecture what he thought about their vaguely responsive reaction to the photo, and his reply was that he didn't remember me showing a photo of a lynching with two or three black individuals in the crowd.

Could it be that the sight of a lynching in the twenty-first century has become so racialized that even when presented with pictures that present a clear exception to its normalcy, we impulsively view them within the white/black binary construct of whites victimizing blacks? I am not suggesting that the blacks represented in the photo set out that day to join in the American ritual of executing another black man, however, reconstructing a plausible explanation for their presence is problematic.

An estimated crowd of 15,000 look on as Jesse Washington is burned alive.
Photo by Fred Gildersleeve

Engaging lynching photos allows us to visually confront the horrors of lynching within the present context of authority and punishment in the United States. Through revisiting the trajectory of antiblack discipline and punishment over the past three centuries, with particular emphasis on the period between Reconstruction and the present, we invariably gain clarification on the present uses of the death penalty. It also might help us make clearer sense of the astonishingly disproportionate number of black men executed in the United States, and shed light on other highly racialized statistics that characterize the criminal justice system, surveillance, and extralegal policing within the United States.

The historical moment captured by Gildersleeve's camera illuminates an even more telling issue: how blacks have come to dichotomize the uses of the death penalty from the historical setting of state-sanctioned lynching while in fact the two are intricately related. Contemporary black responses to the uses of the death penalty must be interrogated, and Gildersleeve's infamous photo, or rather the six photos taken as a whole, provides us with a starting point to examine the above issue.

In revisiting the cultural, political, and social history of punishment in the United States, we find no clear-cut shifts from punishment by hanging (as a spectacle and ritual); to the use of the electric chair (as a substitute), to the present uses of lethal injection (as a ritual). Instead, there has been a consistent and singular race and class rationale shaping the entire trajectory of the development of capital punishment in the United States. When the United States government finally took a stand against the premodern form of antiblack punishment depicted through Gildersleeve's photograph, it had simultaneously taken over the enterprise of killing black bodies as a ritual.

Multiple assumptions invariably ensue when African American people view lynching photos: first, the individual hanging from the tree was unjustly victimized; second, we know (intuitively assume) that the perpetrators were people identifying themselves as white. We view lynching as an activity carried out within the exterior of the legal apparatus, although some of us assume the law officialdom was probably present in some form or capacity. Numerous historians describe scenes of lawlessness, of law enforcement officers being overcome by the overwhelming pressures of mobs. Yet, if we return to Gildersleeve's photo, we will notice that of all the men wearing Stetsons, or similarly branded hats, there is one exception; clearly, one is wearing a law-enforcement hat and is standing in the crowd, laughing and making no apparent effort to stop the lynching. Despite the stillness of the photograph, his expression gives away any pretension of coercion. We should not be surprised at his behavior; as is the case in most any public lynching, we should assume—we can reasonably assume—law officials were aware.

For those of us who probe further into the connotation of these photos, rarely is the innocence of the victims questioned. In other words, rarely do we contextualize lynching as an act of punishment carried out against the historical backdrop of law and order. There is a photograph of a victim's burned corpse, and "Burning of the negro who killed Jim Mitchell—August 10" is written beneath.[2] Did the man kill Jim Mitchell? Was he guilty of murder? The librarian, for example, suggested that it was morally wrong to equate the barbarism of lynching with state-sponsored executions, or to in anyway insinuate that blacks were ever complicit, that they would involve themselves in the act.

Similar to slavery, which in modern times has become associated with blackness, lynching has a history that extends much earlier than the period of modernity, yet at the present historical moment serves as a trope for the enduring legacy of black victimization. When Supreme Court Justice Clarence Thomas's nomination before the Senate Judiciary Committee in 1991 appeared unpromising, his "race card" was simply: "This is a circus.... It's a national disgrace. From my standpoint as a black American, it is a high-tech lynching for uppity blacks who in any way deign to think for themselves." Given the context in which Thomas's words were spoken, they reveal a startling awareness on his part of the technological course of legal lynching. The shameless ease, however, in which he expropriates black suffering, demonstrates how subjectively synonymous with blackness the word "lynching" is and how loosely vulnerable it has become to political commoditization.

While oftentimes the word "lynching" surfaces in response to the media's negative portrayal of African American male celebrities, hardly ever is this rhetoric employed by social commentators when describing the circumstances of Anglo American males similarly attacked by the media. Actually, the origin of the word itself might date back to the beginning of the nineteenth century, to William Lynch, a planter and justice of the peace in Pittsylvania, Virginia. As justice of the peace, Lynch would often take it upon himself to set up unofficial tribunals to try suspects; eventually his method of administering justice was termed *Lynch's law* (later lynch law). Or, perhaps it originates with the Quaker justice of the peace, Charles Lynch, who in 1780 arrested and held captive several individuals for attempting to steal property from the Continental Army. After the war ended, the incarcerated individuals sued Lynch, claiming they had been held illegally. However, in October 1782 an act was passed by the Virginia Sate Legislature justifying Charles Lynch's action, arguing that although the measures taken by him were unlawful, they were justified because of the "imminence of the danger."

No matter the origin, during the burgeoning period of westward expansion lynch law was very popular, as numerous communities had not yet become fully incorporated into the nation-state. With no courts and official judges to immediately call upon to mediate law and order, so-called justice was taken directly into the hands of the citizenry (vigilantes). Lynch law, the punishment of presumed crimes or offenses usually by death without due process of law, was common throughout the United States but reigned supreme in the South and West.

It was not until the period between the last quarter of the nineteenth and early twentieth centuries that "lynching" became exclusively synonymous with black bodily presence. This was particularly the case within the locale of the former Confederate States. Thus, in the broader scope of historical lynching, the practice was not uniquely aimed at African Americans. Commoners, eccentrics, agitators, revolutionaries, witches, heretics, and eventually abolitionists, Mexican Americans, Chinese, and European immigrants, were lynched. Nevertheless, despite the fact that some writers and historians have tried to situate antiblack lynching within this broader context, there are clear distinctions to be made; mainly that the lynching of blacks was a means of terrorizing an oppressed group, suppressing their political and economic aspirations, reaffirming and reinforcing their group marginalization from the mainstream of "society," and it was carried out in pogrom fashion.

The line between extralegal and legal was blurred at best, and eventually the lynching of African Americans became institutionalized within the criminal justice system as a form of ultimate punishment.

LYNCHING TO PROTECT WHITE WOMEN

Mary Jane Brown notes in the introduction to her very important study of women's participation in the antilynching movement, *Eradicating This Evil,* that lynching was a mechanism used by white authorities to reinforce white supremacy, to maintain the highly racialized boundaries of race and place during the advent of Reconstruction. But as black gains from Reconstruction all but vanquished, a new rationale was constructed: the protection of the white woman.

> With protection of women as the excuse for lynching black men, lynching ceased to become a quick execution and became a means of sending a message to black southerners with the lynch mob sometimes even pinning notes of warning to other African Americans to the victim's body. The event became a fearsome public spectacle that signified white community consensus.[3]

However, black-on-white rape was seldom the case. Most often the crime attributed to a state-sanctioned lynching was murder. This point was brought to light in Ida B. Wells's essay *Red Record,* which went a long way toward countering the myth that lynching was carried out in protection of white women. Acknowledging that at least some of the lynching victims had committed crimes, beyond the issue of the brutality itself, she condemned the obvious racism that shaped decisions of who would be lynched. "We have associated too long with the white man not to have copied his vices as well as his virtues. But we do insist that the punishment is not the same for both classes of criminals."[4]

I sense a hint of mockery in her words, but my central point here is that Wells recognized that lynching was popularly viewed by whites as a form of punishment because this is how the issue was framed. She realized that lynching was not a spontaneous, irrational outburst of racial insanity, but instead a carefully deliberated and well-systematized form of antiblack punishment sanctioned by the white community. Compelled by what she referred to as an "unwritten law," whites as a group/class—backed by the state—policed African Americans as a racial underclass. Those blacks who "deigned to think for themselves" were punished.

Black criminality was a widely assumed fact of life, thus Wells sought to reverse the discourse on lynching by emphasizing the criminality of the lynchers (which included the state). The political climate in which she emerged as a national leader was incredibly reactionary, and most national civil rights leaders, politicians, and religious leaders subscribed to some extent to the myth of black criminalization. Historian William S. McFeely acknowledges the role she played in taking on such racial notions and the social context in which she emerged. Commenting on Frederick Douglass's article, "Lynch Law in the South," which was published in the July 1892 issue of *North American Review*, he notes:

> The analysis was acute, but Douglass offered no solution beyond calls for a Southern change of heart—"Let the press and the pulpit unite ... against the cruelty"—and for an "emphatic condemnation and withering reproach" from the North. What was more, his article did not fully disavow the widely accepted assumption that the victims of the horrible executions were to blame for their fate, that black men were indeed a sexual threat to Southern white women. It took a Southern black woman[Ida B. Wells] to fully discredit such an idea.[5]

Douglass's initial reactionary outlook on lynching was tempered by his association with Wells, but this was not the case with Booker T. Washington, the "Wizard of Tuskegee." As Lynda O. McMurry points out in *To Keep the Waters Troubled: The Life of Ida B. Wells*, "Although they agreed on much, her long-held idea of lynching as a white tool to prevent black advancement could not coexist comfortably with his idea that black success brought white acceptance."[6]

Washington was the apostle of accommodation, and ran Tuskegee Institute—an educational institution located on the site of a former plantation—like a modern-day prison industrial complex or plantation; whereas W.E.B. DuBois's notion of a "talented tenth," and later "guiding one-hundredth," implied that the majority of blacks were not ready to fully participate as citizens in the sphere of public life. The level of influence wielded by Washington was unprecedented and hitherto unsurpassed by contemporary leaders. Yet, as Houston Baker, Jr. makes note of in his critically important work, *Turning South Again: Re-thinking Modernism/Re-reading Booker T.*, Washington functioned as a racially subservient leader who managed the affairs of Tuskegee within the framework of the southern mind, that is, of the plantation South. "This plantation was brokerage ground for Booker T.'s own personal power, wealth, and influence over national 'Negro affairs'.... Washington fashioned himself as one of white America's best champions of infinite deferral ('all deliberate speed') of black citizenship and southern public sphere rights for the black masses."[7]

The ideas espoused by Washington, no doubt, trickled down into the consciousness of various African American leaders throughout the country, and in fact, his ideology of gradual racial uplift, with its mantra of servility, instructs contemporary leadership and its role in managing race relations.

LYNCHING AS A LEGAL APPARATUS

The simultaneity of the two words, "lynch" and "law," might even seem to erase any delineation between extrajudicial and legal sanction, and make an exception to the term "due process of law." This is because the act of punishment (to put to death, *usually*[8]) increasingly occurred within the confines of the legal apparatus, and when applied to blacks, the pervasive atmosphere of intimidation throughout the nation and white supremacy hegemony in the post-Confederate South virtually precluded impartial court procedure.

For the present discussion, I would like the readers to view lynching as an act carried out within the confines of the legal apparatus. In doing so we can more accurately synthesize the images we collectively share of black bodies (victims) hanging from trees, or mangled, or being dragged through the street within the present context in which people—some of whom are innocent of the crime—are routinely murdered by the state. We are able to make some sense of photographs depicting groups of people posing for photographs—not something one would do if committing a "crime." We are aware of the numerous individuals lynched by white citizens; of the reign of terror implemented by the Ku Klux Klan during Reconstruction.

We have an historical awareness of such lynchings. But to witness a photo of a lynching, in my view, is another issue—in part: one, it takes place within a certain period after Reconstruction, most likely within the social and political context of early twentieth-century modernity; and two, by the time the photographing of lynching became a part of the ritual, the state was systematically involved. But my ultimate concern is to interpret the presence of those African Americans I see standing in the photo as Jesse Washington is executed.

As a victim of a lynching, not only was one hanged, but his or her body was mutilated, burned, carved into souvenir items, and publicly displayed for the entire community to see. The picture that emerges from the post-Civil War South, at least in the minds of many Americans, is vividly evoked through Abel Meerpol's steadfast lyrics to the song, *Strange Fruit*: "...Black bodies swinging in the Southern breeze, strange fruit hanging from the popular trees..." During the period in history when the late jazz singer Billie Holiday first sang the song, the imagery of black bodies hanging from trees was fresh in the minds of the public, but even today—half a century later—haunting memories are invoked.

That is why for most of us viewing Gildersleeve's photo, the presence of these black individuals raises several troubling questions; that is, if one recognizes them at all. Why were they present? When? How? Why wasn't he lynched in the dark? As Jesse Washington's body lay there defenseless, why weren't those blacks in attendance depicted fighting their way through the crowd to get to him—rescue him—even if it would undoubtedly cost them their lives in this particular instance? Or had they tried to and simply given up after realizing their attempts to intervene were pointless?

Of all the individuals captured in the panorama of Gildersleeve's camera lens, only one individual seems to be visibly disturbed—though we are not certain this is the case. That is to say, one of the black men has his body turned slightly away from the direction where the body is located, looking back over his shoulder in a manner that demonstrates displeasure at the site of Washington being lynched. Yet he also seems oblivious to the crowd around him; doesn't appear to be endangered. There is at least one individual facing him, and he could be standing between the man and Jesse Washington. But, overall, the crowd is focused on Washington, not the other blacks. This isn't a race riot.

Possibly, these individuals were given the responsibility of witnessing the lynching so they could deliver the news to the black community. Perhaps they were family members who would bear the responsibility of not only witnessing the lynching but identifying the body and giving him a proper burial. Maybe they were forced to witness his lynching; after all, this was not an uncommon form of punishment during the antebellum period. Not surprisingly, this is the most common off-the-top-of-your-head explanation I have heard.

These are all unlikely reasons, however, because we know that Les Stegall, an area constable, retrieved Washington's remains and delivered them to an undertaker for burial. They weren't there as bearers of the bad news either, because once the lynching had taken place, some men from the mob took on the responsibility of placing Washington's burned corpse into a cloth bag and dragging it behind an automobile through downtown Waco into the black section of neighboring Robinson, where the remainder of his body was hung from a pole in front of a blacksmith's shop so everyone would be able to see it. So there was no need for them to alert the black community or tell them about what had occurred.

Despite the inexplicable barbarism we see exhibited in the photo, it does not capture the full horrific scenario of events that took place on May 16, 1916. For one, we are safely secure of the loud and rancorous "rebel" yells, the sound of uncouth bodies maneuvering for a better view, the awful stench of thousands gathered in the sweltering Texas heat in such close proximity to one another—the unpleasant odor of the teenager's burned flesh. Though we can certainly conjecture, it is impossible to imagine what Washington sees or sense what he is feeling while young children—children who should be in class, or at least enjoying their lunch break—trade punches over pieces of his bodily parts that have now become strangely recommoditized and made for sale.

To be sure, by the time the lynching had taken place the crowd some estimated at over 15,000 had been whipped into an unconstrained frenzy. And yet, in the face of the mayhem that ensued, there was a chilling method in motion that bears an eerie resemblance to the seemingly more subtle system employed today to carry out state-sanctioned executions. Jesse Washington was *legally* lynched by the state of Texas. His execution was sanctioned, for the most part, by the entire Waco community. Underscoring the entire episode was the specter of racism and white supremacy, but on the surface (as brutal as the scene looks today) it was a ritual as routine as a Friday night football game; or, perhaps a better analogy would be the legal executions that take place regularly in Huntsville, Texas.

An anecdote offered by the venerable theologian Howard Thurman in his book, *The Luminous Darkness*, captures the paradox that oftentimes characterized the response of African American leadership to antiblack terror:

> When I was a student in Atlanta, a blind Negro was
> killed by a policeman. Feelings ran high all through

the Negro community. When his funeral was held,
officers of the law, fearing that it would be an occasion for some kind of uprising, came to the service
but remained outside the church. In his sermon, the
minister had only words of consolation to give to the
family. In his prayer to God, he expressed his anger
and hostility toward the white community. He could
do this in prayer without exposing the Negro community to retaliation.[9]

If it is true, as often stated, that white supremacy has its own logic,
the same holds true of black responses to it. But I would consider
such a response to be a form of protest, particularly considering
the restrictions or imprisoned-like conditions under which such
sentiments were articulated. As an aside, Thurman makes a note
of how the church's role in the civil rights movement eventually
made it a target of racial violence. Yet, written accounts of the
reaction to the lynching of Washington make very little mention
of such sermons.[10] In fact, the community's leadership, we are
told, was very accommodating.

Again, some people will be offended by my argument; they'll
insist that to link the racialized lynching of victims to state-sanctioned executions of individuals who have usually committed
heinous acts of crime is highly inappropriate. Too often, though,
lynching photos are unaccompanied by narratives; they are not
seen as acts of public judgment, as executions carried out within
the confines of the legal apparatus at the given time and place.
Instead, they are looked upon as random and disorderly violence
compelled by uncontrollable racism; or worse, they are simply
seen in no context at all. But during the period in which Washington was lynched, such scenes of subjection were remarkably
consistent: An individual was accused of a crime (sometimes
rape and/or murder; sometimes for venturing outside their
politically subjugated racial boundaries). The police or sheriff
apprehended them, they were quickly tried in a court of law, and
they were convicted. Shortly thereafter, announcements were

made through the media, the news was widely spread, and in a carnival-like atmosphere the victim was lynched.

THE CIRCUMSTANCES LEADING TO JESSE WASHINGTON'S LYNCHING

May 8, 1916, on a farm six miles outside Robinson, Texas, the body of a fifty-three-year-old white woman, Lucy Fryer, was found bludgeoned to death in front of her family's seed shed. Washington, a seventeen-year-old neighbor, worked for the Fryers as a farmhand and right away became the primary suspect. When Sheriff Samuel Fleming found Washington at his home, he was sitting on the front porch cutting a piece of wood. After being taken into custody, Washington at first denied hurting Fryer, but later, after being interrogated (it is difficult to imagine him not being tortured), we are told he confessed to the murder, and even informed the authorities of where the weapon had been hidden.

The following day more than 150 men from Robinson assembled. They did not mount horses; instead they crammed inside thirty automobiles and quietly drove into Waco in search of Washington. However, by the time of their arrival he had already been taken to a neighboring county. When the group of men realized where he was located, the authorities had already moved him again to Dallas, Texas, where he gave a second confession. At this point, it was clear that in order for Washington to be lynched by these individuals, he would have to be brought back to Waco. Through some political maneuvering between the authorities and the group of men, Washington was brought back to Waco to stand trial on Monday, May 15.

The courtroom was so overcrowded that the jury, which included a murderer with a suspended sentence, could barely squeeze into their seats. The trial was over in a matter of hours, around 11:22 A.M. Amazingly, when looking at it from the perspective of the present, the jury took four minutes to reach their verdict. No sooner than it was read the crowd of onlookers proceeded to carry out Washington's punishment in broad daylight.

There was nothing unique regarding the manner in which Washington's legalized lynching took shape, it just happened that Fred Gildersleeve photographed it, commoditized it. But as historians we should, if possible, always learn the story behind these photos because they keep us from viewing lynching in abstract terms. It should be noted that had Washington not been taken out of the courtroom by the lynch mob after the verdict was handed in, he would have no doubt been executed within a few hours, maybe the following day.

Whether any of the victims we see in lynching photos were ever actually guilty of committing heinous crimes in the manner they were accused is uncertain—it is more likely at least some were. We do not condone the punishment of lynching today because of the obvious racial overtones. For rarely, if ever, has a photographer captured a scene that included a white person being victimized by an African American lynch mob—rarely, if ever, do we see black people in such crowds. But these individuals, particularly the one's seen in photos—when photos became readily available to the public—were usually charged with crimes, and in many instances the entire community, both black and white, knew what the punishment would be if they found themselves, or even one of their community's own, justifiably or falsely accused; the ritual was collectively understood. Thus, blacks and whites negotiated the terrains of race and place accordingly. White on black terrorism was tolerated. Blacks lived under a martial law existence by day. By night, they subscribed to a racial curfew.

NAACP AND THE LYNCHING

The National Association for the Advancement of Colored People (NAACP), in its own investigation of the events surrounding the lynching, suggested Washington had attacked Mrs. Fryer after she scolded him for beating a team of mules.

> As Mrs.[Fryer] was scooping[cotton seeds] up for him into the bag which he held, she scolded him for beating the mules. He knocked her down with a blacksmith's

hammer, and, as he confessed, criminally assaulted her; finally he killed her with the hammer. The boy then returned to the field, finished his work, and went home to the cabin, where he lived with his father and mother and several brothers and sisters.[11]

Soon after Washington's arrest, the charge of rape was also added to the crime of murder and news spread quickly to the surrounding towns, and even here the NAACP's report appears to accept at face value the accounts given by the authorities in Waco:

> There was some, but not much doubt of his guilt. The confessions were obtained, of course under duress, and were, perhaps, suspiciously clear, and not entirely in the boy's own words. It seems, however, probably that the boy was guilty of murder, and possibly of premeditated rape.[12]

As late as 1993, historian David Levering Lewis casually comments on Washington's guilt: "The young victim was a mentally impaired field hand who, after raping and killing his white employer's wife in the kitchen, returned to hoe cotton placidly beside the husband, son, and daughter."[13]

The NAACP and other black leaders at the time might have agreed with the Waco authorities that Washington was guilty (or perhaps they did not[14]) but publicly they chose to place sole emphasis on the manner in which he had been lynched, and they also felt strongly that he didn't receive a fair trial. The civil rights organization situated Washington's lynching at the heart of more than one hundred other reported lynchings of African Americans that took place the previous year and used it to launch a crusade against what it referred to as "modern barbarism." Nevertheless, their report, *The Waco Horror*, which owed much to Elisabeth Freeman's investigation, accepted Washington's presumed guilt at face value.

Perhaps there were several investigative journalists willing and able to inquire of the events, but such an assignment would have been far too dangerous to carry out; the individual would no doubt have been beaten or, if lucky, allowed to leave town barely alive. We are left primarily with the results of Freeman's investigation. Employing methods reminiscent of those used by Wells to produce her seminal *Red Record* two decades earlier, the Anglo American suffragist traveled to Waco and gathered testimonies, photographs, and other raw material. *Crisis* editor W.E.B. DuBois then crafted the body of information into a compelling narrative, "The Waco Horror," which appeared as an eight-page supplement to the July 1916 issue of *Crisis* magazine and was distributed to its 42,000 subscribers; given to all the U.S. Congress members; and sent to more than 750 newspapers and more than 500 prominent artists and activists.

There was some dissent. The black editor of the *Paul Quinn Weekly*, A. T. Smith, was arrested and convicted of criminal libel after he printed allegations that Fryer's husband was the real murderer. But there was no mention of Smith in the NAACP's account. Nor is there any mention of the African Americans in attendance. Hubert Harrison, the towering black Harlem socialist, related the events in Waco to an August 23 incident in Houston, Texas, involving African American troops stationed there. Because these soldiers refused to submit to the racial boundaries of Jim Crow and segregation, tensions mounted between them and the white authorities. The soldiers endured arrests, insults, and constant surveillance as they carried out their assignments as guards for the construction of Camp Logan.

On August 23, a black soldier intervened when an African American woman was beaten by two white policemen. He was arrested and assaulted, and when an African American corporal named Charles Baltimore of the Third Battalion inquired about the situation, he was also beaten and arrested. Worse, rumors of his death at the hands of the police were quickly spread. Several of the soldiers marched into downtown Houston, and what followed was a battle in which two black soldiers were killed. But those on the other side of the racial conflict suffered greater casualties: Seventeen deaths, five of them policemen, and twelve others were wounded. Harrison would write:

> Houston and Waco are both in Texas, and both have had killings. At the Waco killing 15,000 people enjoyed themselves while a helpless Negro was put in an iron cage and roasted to death. His eyes were gouged out, and nameless horrible mutilation was practiced on him before thousands of white women and children.
>
> Just about a year later comes the Houston killing. In this one, whites were the sufferers and Negroes the perpetrators. While the first killing was being staged, Negro soldiers were dying at Carizal, Mexico, in[defense] of Texas. Today those Negro soldiers are in Texas, and they have staged a killing on their own account. Both killings were illegal. But every fool knows that the spirit of lawlessness, mob violence and race hatred which found expression in the first was the thing which called forth the second. Negro soldiers (disguise it how we will) must always be a menace to any state which lynches Negro civilians.[15]

Harrison's words were written shortly before the largest military courts-martial in American history would take place. His perspective departs from the traditional narrative of resistance to antiblack terror in that self-defense or armed rebellion is advocated. In his very important autobiography, *Black Bolshevik*, Harry Haywood wrote about his military experience at Camp Logan five days after the rebellion. It is worth quoting at length:

> We were greeted by our comrades from Company G of our battalion on arriving at Camp Logan. They had been there at the time of the mutiny-riot and gave us a detailed account of what had happened. We expected to be confronted by the hostile white population, but to our surprise, the confrontation with the Twenty-fourth seemed to have bettered the racial climate of

this typical Southern town. Houston in those days was a small city of perhaps 100,000 people, not the metropolis it has now become. The whites, especially the police, had learned that they couldn't treat all Black people as they had been used to treating the local Blacks.

I can't remember a single clash between soldiers and police during our six-month stay in the area. On the contrary, if there were any incidents involving our men, the local cops would immediately call in the military police. There was also a notable improvement in the morale of the local Black population, who were quick to notice the change in attitude of the Houston cops. The cops had obviously learned to fear retaliation by Black soldiers if they committed any acts of brutality and intimidation in the Black community.

Houston Blacks were no longer the cowed, intimidated people they had been before the mutiny. They were proud of us and it was clear that our presence made them feel better. A warm and friendly relationship developed between our men and the Black community. The girls were especially proud of us. Local Blacks would point out places where some notorious, nigger-hating cop had been killed.[16]

In all, more than sixty-four African American soldiers were charged in the first of four trials: Five were acquitted, four convicted of lesser charges, forty-two handed life sentences, and thirteen were sentenced to die. These men were summarily hanged on the morning of December 11, even before their sentences were publicly announced. In the three trials that followed, sixteen men were sentenced to death. Six of these men were hanged while twelve were given life sentences.

Haywood's firsthand account of the aftermath is telling, for it confirms the striking poignancy of Harrison's commentary and provides us with a more realistic portrayal of the surround-

ing events as we reexamine black responses to state-sponsored
terror and attempt to understand the real motive forces of social
change. Oftentimes black militancy is erased from our history of
black freedom struggle by revisionist opportunists. These individuals seek to erase radicalism from the narrative of struggle for
a variety reasons—a subject to be taken up elsewhere. Looking
back, however, we must begin to rethink our historiography of
black responses to white terrorism so that black radicalism is seen
in its proper historical light.

Again, from what we are told of Washington's execution,
there was no militant response to it; instead, the NAACP
mounted a public campaign. But as I began to read narratives of
other executions taking place during the period of Washington's,
I came across one that might be of assistance in further clarifying
the action of those in Gildersleeve's photo.

During the spring of 1927, thirteen percent of the land in
Arkansas was covered by floodwaters. More than 210,000 people
were homeless and either living in Red Cross camps or receiving assistance from other sources. The state would not be able
to recover from the disaster without assistance from around the
country. During the months of April and May, the flood was
the main story in the Little Rock newspapers, and other media
throughout the country also focused attention on the flood.
Another event, however, would eventually cast an incandescent
darkness over the floodwaters of Arkansas.

In April, Floella McDonald, a twelve-year-old Anglo American girl, disappeared without a trace. Hers followed the disap-
pearance of a young Little Rock boy a day earlier, although the
police had concluded he simply ran off with a friend. But with
Floella a more thorough search party was organized. Through
rumor, the two missing cases were linked together, and the
Arkansas Democrat printed a story suggesting the children had
been abducted by an African American.

Not until the last day of April, a Saturday, was McDonald's decomposed body discovered in the belfry of a church building after Frank Dixon, the church's African American janitor, informed them of an odor. Dixon, however, became the primary suspect, and he, his son, Lonnie Dixon, as well as six other African Americans, were arrested the same day. Several African Americans were questioned, but the investigators focused their attention on Dixon because they claimed a bloody hat, torn trousers, and gloves belonging to Dixon were found hidden in the church. Further, they claimed an eight-year-old Anglo American girl testified Dixon had kidnapped her near the church a few weeks earlier. Despite the rumors circulating linking the two disappearances, the police carried out their investigation as if they were not. Initially, Frank and Lonnie Dixon denied any involvement in the Floella McDonald murder.

Church services were cancelled the following day, Sunday, but a huge crowd gathered at a cemetery to mourn her death. Certainly most of those in attendance, if not the entire crowd, had already made up their minds who the guilty parties were (the newspapers had already condemned Dixon and his son), and were demanding swift justice—a lynching as it were. However, the Reverend J.O. Johnson cautioned them, "A lynching right now, when the attention of the nation is focused on Arkansas as a result of the flood situation, would cause irreparable harm to the reputation of the state. I beseech you to leave the matter to the courts." In other words, instead of lynching Frank and Lonnie Dixon, they should allow the state to legally lynch them.

Across town, the police obtained a confession from Lonnie Dixon that he raped and killed the girl. Although meticulous in their use of interrogation techniques such as sleep deprivation, physical coercion, and threats of violence to other African Americans—namely his father—they neglected to write down his confession. Despite being exonerated, the father was held because it was assumed he had knowledge of the crime. The news of Dixon's confession traveled widely and quickly, and the following day, authorities were already being quoted as saying he would get the "electric chair," as Arkansas's law allowed children as young as fourteen to be executed.

While Arkansas was perhaps drenched in racial conflict, the antiblack mobilization around this issue was unprecedented. What was the response of African American leadership? In the case of Jesse Washington, we are left with Gildersleeve's photo. Regardless of what we assume, we are ultimately forced to rely upon numerous conjectural uncertainties. However, the response of African American leadership in Little Rock reveals a pattern and forces us to reconsider the presence of those in Waco, and ultimately illuminates much-needed clarity on contemporary responses of African American leadership to legal lynching.

According to Brian Greer, the writer whose narrative I've borrowed, "The Association of Negro Ministers of All Denominations issued a resolution praising police for their efforts to apprehend Lonnie Dixon. On behalf of the 'negro population of Little Rock and vicinity,' the ministers condemned the 'dastardly crime committed and confessed by a youth of our race in this community' and asked for a 'speedy trial and legal punishment if found guilty.'"[17] Perhaps their reason for issuing the statement was to curtail the broader racial conflict looming on the horizon. After all, it is 1927, and the state has now taken over the process of executing African Americans. In this case, there was an all-out effort on the part of the authorities to simultaneously ensure antiblack vengeance and prohibit mob action. Also, perhaps these African American leaders were coerced into issuing the statement; again, the world is watching.

Editorials ran heaping praises on the police for the superb job they had done in curtailing an imminent lynching. The following day, Lonnie Dixon was indicted on charges of murder and rape; the death penalty would be sought by the prosecuting authorities. Once again, the flood was making the headlines. The next day, however, two Anglo American women claimed to have been attacked by a 38-year-old African American man named John Carter; the citizens of Little Rock would have their lynching. Several African American men attempted to join the search party, calling the sheriff to offer their assistance: "At noon, nine of the city's black leaders... called the sheriff to offer their assistance. They were clearly trying to head off a lynching." (p. 5) Among this group was lawyer Scipio Africanus Jones, a prominent African American political figure in Little Rock who had gained national notoriety defending 12 black men involved in a "race war" a decade earlier in Elaine, Arkansas. On the surface, their behavior might seem to make sense; they are simply attempting to diffuse a potential full-scale racial conflict. Again, little historical analysis has been preserved that explains the presence of those African Americans watching Washington's lynching. But from these other narratives such as that of John Carter's we are able to frame an analysis of the relationship between African American leadership and antiblack discipline and punishment.

In the aftermath of a lynching, it was not uncommon for black civic and religious leaders to voice their support and to join the white community leaders in condemning the crime. In one instance, Bob Davis was lynched by both whites and at least one black person (a woman) after being accused of assaulting both a white shopgirl and the black women's daughter, a teenager. According to Philip Dray, in his book *At the Hands of Person's Unknown: The Lynching of Black America,*

> The mother of the black girl who had been assaulted was given the *privilege* of firing the first shot at Davis, who had been bound to a tree. With a crowd of armed white men behind her offering advice and encouragement, the mother stood several paces from the prisoner, took aim at his midsection, and squeezed the trigger. The crowd then joined in, its fusillade blowing Davis into pieces.[18]

But this type of multiracial lynching is rarely seen in photos and certainly was a rare event. Dray acknowledges that oftentimes—and I would think more often than not—"agreeing after

the fact that a lynching had been good and proper was also a
sound survival strategy...." Perhaps the black people pictured in
Gildersleeve's photo were friends of the Fryers, and were there to
see justice carried out. Although I am merely speculating, I sense
that their presence at the lynching was a sign of accommodation,
a means of making peace with the Anglo American community.

Washington's lynching took place during a period when the
highly racialized spectacle of lynching was becoming more centralized and vigilantism was being publicly shunned in favor of
a racialized system of white supremacy law and order. Washington, like Carter a decade later, stood between two worlds: one in
which vigilantism reigned supreme, where the state had not fully
incorporated its citizenry into its post-World War II law-and-order
hegemony; the other in which the state assumed the responsibility
of maintaining a system of antiblack vengeance, public spectacle,
and ritual, and promoting an image of democracy and progress all
at once. The so-called trial of Washington was itself a lynching. It
was driven by the white community's antiblack psychosis resulting from the history of slavery in this country. Once slavery ended,
other means had to be developed to maintain a system of antiblack
discipline and punishment. In such an environment we find the
origins of the present uses of the death penalty and the racialized
criminal justice system in which it was implemented.

DISENFRANCHISEMENT OF BLACKS

Accommodationist African American leadership relied
heavily on the idea of legislative justice, for what other means
did they have at their disposal to combat their racially terrorized
conditions? By the second decade of the twentieth century—
when Washington was executed—an elaborate scheme of black
disenfranchisement was legalized throughout all of the former
Confederate states. No African American, not even the "talented
tenth" was completely immune from Jim Crow. This history of
disenfranchisement must have been fresh in the minds of African
American leaders, many of whom were children when in 1883

the Supreme Court ruled that the Civil Rights Act of 1875 was unconstitutional. This law had guaranteed that all persons should be entitled "full and equal enjoyment of accommodations, advantages, facilities, and privileges of inns, public conveyances on land or water, theatres, and other places of public amusement." After reviewing five cases of discrimination, Supreme Court Chief Justice Bradley argued that the Fourteenth Amendment did not apply to private businesses and individuals. Such a ruling by the nation's highest judicial authority ushered in a wave of legislation by southern lawmakers enforcing white supremacy.

In his seminal work, *Race, Racism and American Law*, legal scholar Derrick Bell notes that

> In the post-Reconstruction years, the law failed black people, less because it was inadequate than because when they needed it most for their physical safety, it deserted them entirely. Laws that emasculated the right to vote posed an ominous handicap to their participation in government policymaking; laws that required segregation in public facilities constituted a humiliation to the spirit. But it was the absolute refusal of the law to protect them from random and organized violence that enabled the virtual re-enslavement of a race so recently freed.[19]

For more than half a century after the Civil War ended, African Americans lived under circumstances many have called worse than slavery. Nevertheless, by the turn of the twentieth century African Americans were now enroute, slowly but surely (violated against), into American modernity.

In 1940, at a Tuskegee conference, lynching was defined as such: legal evidence of an illegal death at the hands of groups acting under the pretext of serving justice. Most historians would agree that for most of American history—I would argue throughout the course—the state has been the primary sanctioning body of antiblack terror. Yet, in the face of this irony, the state was called upon by traditional black leadership to redress antiblack terror. By constructing lynching as an act outside the realm of law, African American leadership created for itself both the oppositional space and opportunity to negotiate its newly acquired enlightened ideas on racial uplift in a manner that conformed to the notion of progress. To acknowledge the state's primary role in antiblack discipline and punishment (i.e., public lynching) would have betrayed the promise of legislative and judicial justice in which they had so desperately anchored their hopes.

LYNCHING AND THE DEATH PENALTY

Students of history are often warned to be careful about reading the present into the past, but in the case of the death penalty we should make an exception. After all, it is the most prominent example of how the past intrudes upon the present landscape of authority and punishment. Only after becoming involved in a movement to stop an individual from being executed did I begin to raise serious questions regarding the history of state-sanctioned executions. Prior to such involvement the connections between lynching and the present uses of the death penalty went unrecognized in my political awakening—at best, lynching was simply a metaphor for the death penalty. However, the tragic dramatization of the execution of Shaka Sankofa erased all my doubts about the historical connections (see later in this chapter).

The political behavior of African American leadership leading up to his death cannot be separated from the tragic outcome. I have come to the conclusion that unless African American leadership begins to view antiblack racism, lynching, and capital punishment as aspects of a totality, we will continuously seek ad hoc and spontaneous solutions of no consequence to the broader problems associated with the criminal justice system and the continuing historical role it plays in maintaining black subjugation and disenfranchisement. There needs to be a clearer understanding of what is actually taking place in the United States so that we can began the task of collectively acting on what is to be done.

Perhaps the best way of arriving at an understanding of the nature and purpose of the death penalty is by examining its history of development and focusing attention on the various underlying attributes that have continuously characterized the institution. The historical development of the present uses of the death penalty can be delineated by four periods: (1) slavery (1500-1862); (2) the period of Reconstruction (1863-1888); (3) the period of state-sanctioned legal lynching (1896-1923); and (4) the present period of state-sponsored legal lynching (1924-present). My point here is not to provide an extensive overview of these periods, but to simply highlight the "shifts" in each historical stage leading to the present uses of the death penalty. I strongly feel that antiblackness, fear of black people, continued to be the overriding rationale *shading* the implementation of the death penalty throughout these four periods. Part of what needs to be done is to revisit, reconceptualize, and redefine the meaning of lynching in such a way that it is historically connected to the present uses of the death penalty. In a sense, in order for activists to determine what is to be done, there needs to be clarity on what is being done.

At the heart of any public discussion of lynching and the death penalty in the United States is the concept of due process. Due process, originally phrased "law of the land," was drawn from the Magna Carta (1215) and the concept was transported to the New World as early as 1692, showing up in the Massachusetts statute as "due process of law." Nearly a century later, the Fifth Amendment to the Constitution stated that the federal government could not deprive any person of "life, liberty, or property without due process of law." While it might be true that in the broader scope of history there are clear delineations between lynching and the present uses of the death penalty, it wasn't until 1868—three crucial years after the Civil War ended—that "due process" was extended to the formerly enslaved Africans. Due process of law eluded most enslaved Africans, however, and when the Fourteenth Amendment was enacted, the response of the former slaveholders was to nullify it by instigating a reign of unprecedented terror against the formerly enslaved.

What, then, is lynching? It needs to be defined in a manner that doesn't obscure the complicity of the state. Notwithstanding its formal definition, it is an act of brutal intimidation and social control designed to maintain the social, economic, and political structure of white class privilege; an act of deadly terror against an entire community or class of people; a relationship of power; a symbol of white group power; and above all else, an ultimate form of racial authority over black group powerlessness.

Lynching transcends time and space. For example, black people living in the twenty-first century view lynching photos of the early twentieth century and identify with the victims they know little about, share no social relationship to, and in most instances know or ask nothing of the circumstances that led to the lynching. Finally, for our purposes, lynching is an act whereby one group sacrifices of itself to appease the antiblack psychosis of another group. Lynching was not an act carried out solely by the community's white "ne'er do wells," nor was it solely under the control of the ruling elite. Lynching was a communal activity, a ritual—it involved men, women, and children of all the various white ethnic groups—rich and poor alike. Probably no other activity fostered white community, identity, and solidarity more than the public spectacle of a black person being lynched. Likewise, the continual threat and fear of lynching was shared collectively by the black community. It was a perpetual tool of fear used to govern race and place. Lynching dramatized the raw, brutal, and evident authority whites held over blacks. And just as lynching solidified "white community," it led to the fragmentation of the African American community.[20]

The historian Ira Berlin has suggested that despite being maintained by violence, slavery was a "negotiated relationship."

> To be sure, the struggle between master and slave
> never proceeded on the basis of equality and was

always informed by the master's near monopoly of force. By definition, slaves had less choice than any other people, as slaveholders set the conditions upon which slaves worked and lived. Indeed, the relation between master and slave was so profoundly asymmetrical that many have concluded that the notion of negotiation—often freighted in our own society with the rhetoric of the level playing field—has no value to the study of slavery.[21]

Berlin's observation about race relations within the context of the institution of slavery is equally useful in characterizing the relationship between the black and white communities of the postslavery era. The period of slavery was by far the most violent era of the African American experience, but in some ways the terrorism that came along with the South's attempts to confront the reconfigured dynamics of race and place consequent to its demise reveals an even more unsettling historical moment.

The relationship between lynching and the death penalty is historical and cultural. The present uses of the death penalty sanctions the historical relationship of *authority* that those in power have over the powerless. This authority expresses itself on a symbolic level as well as in practical terms. On the symbolic level, it is highly racialized and reinforces a collective sense of whiteness, even as poor marginalized whites are victimized. On the practical level, lethal injection, and whatever form that coincides with or comes after, is essentially a substitute method (just as the electric chair was a substitute for the use of the rope) of implementing state-sanctioned antiblack terror. The spectacle is then increasingly hidden from the public; white supremacy is allowed to be played out on a symbolic and covert level.

In their study, *The Rope, the Chair, & the Needle: Capital Punishment in Texas, 1923-1990*, Marquart, Ekland-Olson, and Sorensen examined the racialized statistics that shaped each form of punishment in Texas and concluded that the differences between them was essentially a moot point.

The rejection of vigilante justice was facilitated by a broader shift in the definition of "place," in this instance as defined by standing before the law. By expanding the protections of rational-legal due process, encouraged by a more centralized system of capital punishment, the exclusionary beliefs and practices aimed at citizens whose roots were African-American became less stark. This shift in the spectrum of beliefs was, to be sure, a matter of shading rather than sharp contrast. The legacy of an overrepresentation of blacks among the executed population would continue for several decades.[22]

A brief look at the period preceding that in which the electric chair was first used in the South further elucidates their point about the "matter of shading." Prior to 1923, individuals convicted of capital offenses in Texas were executed in the county of their conviction. By then 394 executions had taken place, and the statistics already revealed the racialized context in which they were being administered: an incredible 60 percent were African American; 12 percent were Latino; 26 percent were Anglo; and 5 percent were Native American, although, the number of Native Americans executed per capita was considerably higher. What is even more striking is that 60 percent of the number of African Americans executed took place between the years 1867 and 1899. The political economy of lynching is made obvious by the statistics. But there were cultural factors, too.

David M. Oshinsky, in his book *Worse Than Slavery*, likened public executions to theater: "They had their own cast of characters—the judge, the sheriff, the minister, the grieving families, the condemned—and a common set of scenes." Examining the racism inherent in the Mississippi criminal justice system and the historical relationship between lynching and executions, he notes

the attempt to separate lynchings from legal executions may well be futile, for the line between them is sometimes narrow, at best. Mississippi was among

the last states to abolish public executions and to
bring them under state control. As a result, these
events frequently resembled mob actions in which a
predetermined verdict was followed by a gruesome
carnival of death.[23]

Such narratives are repeated so often one wonders whether they are
not rereading the same scenes of brutal and racialized subjection.
Eventually, forces were mobilized to the point where some reforms
and concessions had to be made. But what type of reforms?

There were several factors that led authorities to reform the
system of administering executions. In Texas, J.W. Thomas began
campaigning on the platform that public hangings should be
removed from the emotional atmosphere of the local communities to a more central location, in Huntsville. Churches, women's
groups, and Christian organizations also took up the cause. Already,
beginning in the 1890s, the peak period, states began removing
these executions from the emotionally charged atmosphere to
more centralized locations. But lynching continued. When in
1921 Representative Leonidus C. Dyer of Missouri introduced
the House bill that would punish the crime of lynching, legislators
from the South immediately mounted intense opposition. According to Mary Frances Berry, author of *Black Resistance, White Law:
A History of Constitutional Racism in America*, "Opponents of the
bill responded that antilynching legislation was an NAACP tactic
to keep black violators from being punished."[24] Between 1921 and
1948 numerous legislative attempts to criminalize lynching followed, but all were similarly rebuffed. The end result remained the
same: lack of real due process; the death of an African American
(a black body, as far as the Anglo public was concerned). However,
the shift away from the public spectacle created a much better environment for African American leadership to advocate the idea of
black citizenship.

In *Speak Now Against the Day*, historian John Egerton points
out that on the average, one person was lynched every month
throughout the entire 1930s decade. Nine out-of-ten times

the victim was African American. But he further reminds us: "Beyond the 'official' statistics on lynching, many additional deaths of blacks at the hands of whites were classified as disappearances or accidents, or as some 'legal' form of homicide such as involuntary manslaughter or self-defense. The end result was the same; death without due process."[25]

There exists a hidden history of lynching in America. Thus, any attempt to frame an analysis of lynching relying on the government statistics will prove gravely inadequate. Readers should not confuse lynching from "legal" lynching, although as I have noted elsewhere, they occur within the same context of white supremacy hegemony. Lynching is an activity carried out regularly, even today. For example, the lynching in Texas in 1998 of James Byrd, Jr.—widely reported by the media as a hate crime—should be considered as an extralegal lynching (see chapter 2 of this book). There are few reliable statistical studies on this aspect of American terrorism, and there is something to be said about how easily anti-black terror is erased from historical memory (i.e., the millions of Africans killed in the Middle Passage, genocide in Rwanda). Public lynching, however, was nearly always sanctioned by the state. Individuals posing in lynching photographs did not fear legal reprisal, as there are virtually no recorded instances of such cases. I see little reason to differentiate between public and legal lynching unless, of course, the public lynching was done solely outside the realm of any pretext of discipline and punishment.

INTRODUCTION OF THE ELECTRIC CHAIR

There is no doubt that the increasing availability of the electric chair helped to move authorities away from usages of public hangings, as it was viewed as a more progressive and humane way of administering an execution. Following a decade of controversy between Thomas A. Edison and George Westinghouse, William Kemmler of New York became the first person executed by electric chair on August 6, 1890.[26] The rivalry between the two leading electrical companies—Edison's General Electric Company and

Westinghouse's Westinghouse Corporation—reached its climax when Edison initiated a massive smear campaign warning the public against the dangers of using AC (alternating current). In 1887, Edison organized a public demonstration in West Orange, New Jersey, where he set up a 1,000 volt Westinghouse generator, attached it to a metal plate, and executed a dozen animals by placing them on the electrified plate.

As northern states began to change their methods of punishment, executions in the South continued to be a spectacle. In 1923 the Texas legislature eventually voted to centralize capital punishment.[27] Marquart, Ekland-Olson, and Sorensen note that this legislative move was primarily motivated by a need to acquiesce to national trends, as well as to respond to several highly racialized spectacles during the preceding years. The centralization of punishment was not in response to attitudinal changes but rather the necessity of concealing the public spectacle.

> The hope was that this new statute would reduce the emotional tension surrounding local hangings and these public spectacles would soon recede into a dimly remembered past. While remnants of this past would continue to show up in ugly detail, by adopting state-controlled electrocutions for more secluded executions, Texas legislators hoped to demonstrate that their state was in greater concord with evolving standards of decency.[28]

The uses of the electric chair as opposed to the rope merely allowed authorities to carry out executions in less visible and more highly technical fashion. Although as violent as the uses of the rope, the electric chair was touted as a more humane substitute.

For execution by the electric chair, the person was usually shaved and strapped to a chair with belts that crossed their chest, groin, legs, and arms. A metal skullcap-shaped electrode was attached to the scalp and forehead over a sponge moistened with saline. It was important that the sponge not be too wet or the saline short-circuited the electric current, as it would then have had a very high resistance. An additional electrode was moistened with conductive jelly (Electro-Creme) and attached to a portion of the prisoner's leg that had been shaved to reduce resistance to electricity. The prisoner was then blindfolded. U.S. Supreme Court Justice William Brennan described electrocutions:

> The prisoner's eyeballs sometimes pop out and rest on[his] cheeks. The prisoner often defecates, urinates, and vomits blood and drool. The body turns bright red as its temperature rises, and the prisoner's flesh swells and his skin stretches to the point of breaking. Sometimes the prisoner catches fire.... Witnesses hear a loud and sustained sound like bacon frying, and the sickly sweet smell of burning flesh permeates the chamber.[29]

This scene was enacted in the movie *The Green Mile* (1999), directed by Frank Darabont. The fictional movie dramatizes the lives of death-row prison guards, and the narrative leads up to the execution of a wrongly accused African American man who has the power to heal. Darabont includes three execution scenes in the movie, and in each he focuses the camera lens on the spectators who are routinely seated in an orderly fashion. Their collective gaze is void of emotion and reveals the continuity of executions as an orderly spectacle. The executioners rehearse the routine as one would any ritual.

The movie's most emotionally disturbing scene takes place midway through, and ends all doubt regarding the humanity of using the electric chair. The villainous character, Percy Wetmore (played by Doug Hutchinson), has set his mind on "frying" a death row inmate. In one of the executions, he places a dry sponge on the victim's head, and what follows is a gruesome scene that haunts the viewers long after they leave the theatre. *The Green Mile* is fictional but the film's depiction of an execution by electric chair was based on real eyewitness accounts.

LYNCHING AND ENSLAVED AFRICAN AMERICANS

There is a growing assumption among many scholars that during the antebellum period the practice of lynching was rarer because enslaved Africans, as a commodity, had greater worth attached to them in a precapitalist economic system.[30] Some anti-death penalty activists point to the fact that in Texas, not since James Wilson, alias Rhode Wilson, was hanged for killing an enslaved African American in 1854 had an Anglo American been executed for murdering an African American in that state. The enslaved African American, named Bill, was the property of Anderson Barkley, and thus, by killing him, an economic blow was dealt to Barkley. Probably the original source for this widely known episode originated in Lou Ella Moseley's *Pioneer Days of Tyler County*, and as she notes, "The cause for the murder was not recorded nor was the owner identified, since there were at least three Anderson Barkley's in the county in the early days."[31] Moseley doesn't speculate why Wilson was executed other than for murder. But I think it would be fundamentally incorrect to assume enslaved Africans had a greater degree of protections due to their circumstances as property, and would rather not focus too much attention on questions of political economy, particularly within the present context. It is, as William S. McFeely pointed out in 1997,

> necessary for us neither to count up the numbers of black Americans who have been killed nor to recount a history of racism. What is important to a discussion of the present-day death penalty is to look at certain uses of violence over the course of American history. The physical pain meted out under slavery and by lynchers had the purpose of creating a psychological fear designed to control a large stretch of black communities. In the past, there were two reasons for exercising that control—the need for labor and fear of the black people who were the laborers. In the 1990s there is no longer the same need for that

labor, but the fear remains. Many in the majority
community, consisting of both the affluent and those
afraid of slipping from economic security, dread not
only black folk, but the poor in general. Desperate
poverty may lead to desperate acts, thus, those who
feel threatened by this desperation use the power of
the state to control those they fear. To exercise that
control, there are increasing calls for and use of the
death penalty.[32]

From the very beginning, the death penalty has been used as
a means of maintaining racial and class authority and mediating
such fears. According to Winthrop D. Jordan, in his book *White
Over Black*, there was a lynching in Roxbury, Massachusetts, in
July 1741. A "Negro" man was accused of stealing money and
tied to a tree, whipped, and laid on the ground before a crowd
of people. "This was communal effort with a vengeance," writes
Jordon, who cites this episode as one of the earliest recorded
lynchings.[33]

Historians John Hope Franklin and Loren Schweninger note
in their book *Runaway Slaves* that enslaved Africans paid a heavy
price for dissenting. And again, the notion that somehow slaves
were treated better because of their value as property is disputed:

> The argument that slaves were not treated harshly
> because they were valuable property ignores the
> conviction among most slave owners and many
> other whites that severe chastisement would serve
> as a deterrent. Those who openly defied the owner,
> plantation manager, or overseer were usually dealt
> with quickly and ruthlessly. They were whipped,
> beaten, cropped, branded, and sometimes tortured.
> They were sold away from their families or watched
> as their children were turned over to slave traders.
> Those found guilty or sometimes merely accused
> of serious "crimes"—arson, assault, rape attempted
> murder, conspiracy, poisoning—were banished or
> hanged.[34]

Peter Irons notes in *A People's History of the Supreme Court,*

> The "black codes" of the South were designed to
> keep slaves "in their place" by force and violence. The
> Virginia legislature passed a law in 1669 that acknowl-
> edged the difficulty of dealing with "the obstinacy of
> many of them by other than violent means" and provided
> that 'if any slave resist his master...and by the extremity of
> the correction should chance to die,' the owner would be
> "acquit from molestation" and suffer no penalty. Southern
> colonists also feared, with some reason, that their slaves
> might plot or actually rebel against their condition. To
> prevent and punish such rebellions, the Virginia legis-
> lature provided in 1723 that "if any number of negroes"
> shall "consult, advise, or conspire, to rebel or make insur-
> rection... they shall suffer death."[35]

The more Africans rebelled against their enslavement, the tighter
the reins of repression, and there was continuous rebellion. Executions were widely employed as a deterrent to rebellion.

IMAGINING CONFEDERACY

Clearly, the origins of the present uses of the death penalty
extend back to the institution of slavery. Nonetheless, following
the Civil War, the rope became an active weapon in the hands of
Confederate secessionists, reaching a fevered peak by the turn of
the century. Lynching became an outlet for disillusioned white
supremacists. Between the years 1882 and 1968, the deaths of
5,000 African American men, women, and children were docu-
mented by the Tuskegee Institute. Yet, as I pointed out earlier,
this doesn't include those cases that went unnoticed.

Sharon Patricia Holland writes in her book, *Raising the Dead,*

> Manumission dictated that the peculiar social status
> of enslaved people be transferred to and shared by
> another space altogether. Not willing to comprehend
> fully the freed state of formally enslaved subjects,
> masters and their kin reserved a special place in their
> imaginations for this new being. Although seeing

the black subject as a "slave" was now prohibited by
law, there was no impediment to viewing this subject
in the same place s/he had always occupied. In this
way the enslaved-now-freed person, either "black" or
close enough to this category, began to occupy the
popular imagination. Ultimately a system such as
slavery might be abruptly halted, but its dream lives
in the peoples' imagination and becomes fodder for
both romantic fictions and horrific realities.[36]

In addition to reformulating a definition of lynching and the
present uses of the death penalty, contemporary discourses on
state sanctioned, extrajudicial and antiblack terror need to be
resituated within the context of their relationships to neo-Confederate ideology. Throughout the South, whether through the
names of businesses, streets, educational institutions, uses of language, historical markers, and other various contestations over
"space," the maintenance of neo-Confederate ideology plays an
integral part in shaping the cultural and architectural landscape
of whiteness. It is through such an antiblack ideology that the
"romantic fictions" Holland reminds us of are maintained.

State-sanctioned executions are all but continuation/reen-
actments of the brutal, sadistic, and rampant murder we've come
to associate with the images in lynching photos most of us have
witnessed. The lethal-injected executions taking place in the U.S.
South, and indeed across the entire nation, clearly place us in
the same historical and political context as that in which Jesse
Washington's legal lynching took place. His execution, and the
thousands of others like it, was carried out within the context of
present-day antiblack discipline and punishment.

It is my belief that African American leadership came to
accept legalized lynching as a form of discipline and punishment because it both erased the highly racialized spectacle of
lynching and allowed them to be spared of association with the
individual(s) accused of the crime. In other words, prior to the
acceptance of an antiblack system of criminal justice, the entire

community was presumed guilty for the crime of one whether they were related by class or family ties. Lynching was usually followed by an assault against entire African American communities. Thus, lynching was unequivocally regarded as a form of collective punishment by both the dominant white society and its victimized African community.

By integrating the gathering of lynchers (the white community), African American leadership was essentially attempting to diffuse or "deracialize" the racialized spectacle. Legal executions also allowed the emergent African American leadership classes the opportunity to marginalize potential armed rebellions on the part of those willing to fight back against white injustices—particularly in self-defense—against lynching activities. This is particularly true between the years 1916 and 1968, as African Americans increasingly gained military experience, access to weaponry, and were radicalized from fighting in wars abroad, increased frustrations with antiblack terror, and basic survival. Throughout the course of the African American experience in America, there have been contestations over leadership representations, and it would be a grave mistake to underestimate how low some would stoop in pursuit of the upper hand in this battle. Thus, it is clear that just as those individuals who publicly supported lynching could rationalize their actions by suggesting they had little choice in the matter, they, on the other hand, could expect to be rewarded with prestige and patronage by the dominant white community. Thus the lure of being accepted within the dominant group must have been an enticement to many of the African American political and business leaders, no different than today when African American leaders endorse the use of the death penalty or, in some instances, simply refuse to publicly articulate their indifferences. Although on the surface it might seem reasonable to assume these individuals were making a rational choice, they were more than likely motivated by protecting their own financial, political, and social interests.[37]

A closer look at Gildersleeve's photo will not only reveal the presence of African Americans on the periphery of the crowd but also close to Washington's body. Standing less than ten feet from the men hoisting Washington's body are two other African American men who, again, do not seem to be endangered; nor are they assisting Washington. Judging by the dress of one, he is prosperous. He is donning a black derby; better dressed than the whites accompanying him. Nonetheless, there is no logical reason for his presence, unless he was there to stop the lynching.

BLACK POWERLESSNESS AND THE CRIMINAL JUSTICE SYSTEM

In 1972, when the Supreme Court declared the death penalty unconstitutional, the reason it gave was that "the death sentence is disproportionately carried out on the poor, the Negro, and the members of unpopular groups." At present, the unsettling racial statistics reveal a continued antiblack and antipeople of color bias. For example, although African-Americans comprise 12 percent of the United States population, they constitute 42 percent of those awaiting execution. Ironically, the jurisdiction with the highest percentage of persons of color on death row is the United States military, where 89 percent of the inmates are nonwhite. In Louisiana, 72 percent of the death row population is nonwhite, but Pennsylvania, a state located in the Northeast, follows close behind with 70 percent of its population being nonwhite—including the influential writer and political prisoner Mumia Abu-Jamal (see Chapter 4 of this book). In fact, in Philadelphia the odds of an African American receiving the death sentence are 38 percent higher than if the individual were Anglo American.

More than 60 percent of juveniles awaiting execution in the United States are either African American or Latino, and two out of three of those executed since the reinstatement of the death penalty in 1976 have been African American or Latino. While the numbers of both African American and Anglo American murder victims are somewhat equal, 80 percent of the persons executed since 1977 were convicted of murdering Anglo American victims. Such startling statistics, while sufficient, do very little to reveal the way in which African Americans are routinely victimized by a racialized system of discrimination. They do little to illustrate the processes of racial discrimination. Consider, for example, that 99 percent of individuals who decide whether an African American will be put to death are white.

My point, however, is to suggest that the present political and social landscape where American citizens are routinely executed by the state mirrors that of the early twentieth century; indeed, there have been no epochal shifts in the administering of antiblack discipline and punishment. The manner in which African Americans are discriminated against in juries, as defendants, and as victims exemplifies their powerlessness within the criminal justice system. And the fact that in most all of the states that still carry out death penalties, politicians—on every level—are beholden to small, well-financed pro-death penalty organizations.

GARY GRAHAM'S (SHAKA SANKOFA'S) EXECUTION

As I mentioned earlier, it was during the winter of 1993 that I became a part of a campaign to halt the execution of Gary Graham, an African American man who had been sentenced to death at the age of seventeen, and who was faced with an execution date. My initial reason for volunteering to work for his campaign was simple: there was an overwhelming amount of evidence to suggest he was innocent of the crime of which he was convicted of. Graham's fate rested on the mistaken identity of an individual eyewitness.

Although eight crime scene witnesses were identified who saw the assailant the night of Bobby Lambert's murder, Bernadine Skillern was the only one who claimed to have seen Graham. Yet, of these eyewitnesses, Skillern had the poorest view of the assailant. She testified that she had a frontal view of the assailant's face for only two or three seconds, at night, from a distance of thirty to forty feet in a dimly lit parking lot.

Once the victim was killed, she claimed to have trailed the assailant in her automobile, only halting after her children in the back seat begged her not to pursue him. While her description of the events following the murder might have been true, they seem quite imaginative. Yet, in the years leading up to Graham's execution, she never recanted her testimony; she never entertained the idea that she could have falsely identified the assailant.

There were other forms of evidence, such as ballistics and witness tampering, that made it very clear this was a case shaped by overwhelming reasonable doubt. For example, it was discovered prior to Graham's execution that the Houston Police Department's ballistics expert found that the .22-caliber gun used to murder Lambert did not match that found in Graham's possession. The prosecutors withheld this evidence from the jury. Needless to say, several jurors later signed affidavits that they would have decided differently had they been shown this evidence. In addition, witnesses—at least five—who were closer to the scene, and who would not identify Graham as the assailant, were never heard from by the jury. As an activist with some level of political consciousness, it wasn't difficult to comprehend the numerous contradictions surrounding his ordeal.

Graham's circumstances seemed to reflect a pattern: as an indigent African American, so horrendous was his court-appointed legal representation, it was questionable whether he was afforded *due process of law*, for in later years, by his attorney's own admission, he believed Graham was guilty and neglected to investigate the evidence of his innocence. The trial took two days with no witnesses called during the guilt phase of the trial, and in his closing remarks the jury was thanked by Graham's attorney, Ronald G. Mock, for sentencing Graham to death. At the time of Graham's execution, six individuals represented by Mock had been executed and five awaited their deaths, and for this there was a wing of the Ellis One prison unit appropriately named by those incarcerated there as the "Mock Wing."

Graham did not receive a fair trial and because of the clemency law in Texas at the time of his trial that prohibited an individual from providing evidence of innocence after thirty days,[38] Graham was never able to receive a fair trial; even though his case was drawn out over a long period of time and he was given five stays of execution.[39] Finally, Graham's struggle was given extensive coverage by both the print and electronic media. He essentially became a "poster boy" for both opponents and proponents of the death penalty in the state of Texas.

In 1996, Gary Graham renamed himself Shaka Sankofa to reflect the growing consciousness he had developed of his African heritage and responsibility. By then, Sankofa had emerged as a revolutionary leader, articulating a radical perspective not only around the issue of the death penalty but on other pressing issues facing the entire African American community. Like numerous other prison intellectuals, Sankofa saw beyond the confines of prison. For him, prison was a starting point for looking at the systematic oppression within the broader society. In my attempt to make sense of the events that led to the legal lynching of Sankofa, I recognized that at every stage of the tragic narrative of his ordeal, he was failed by African American leadership. From the lawyers to the politicians; from the Texas board of pardons and paroles to the Supreme Court, African American leadership failed him in dramatic fashion.

During one of my visits to him at the Ellis One Unit in Huntsville, Texas, in 1996, Sankofa spoke about the clemency process, as well as the Texas Board of Pardons and Paroles.[40] I came away from that visit believing that this body of 18 governor appointees was essentially an all-white version of the white citizens' council or a modern-day vigilante committee. This was my belief up until shortly after Sankofa's death when I was preparing to speak to a group of activists in Dallas, Texas. While preparing my notes, I noticed that many of the members were either African American or Hispanic. It was at this point that I began to examine the compliant participation of African American leadership in the process of legal lynching.

Sankofa's execution was delayed up to nearly three hours because of a last-minute effort on the part of his attorneys to get the Supreme Court to hear his case. As more than 200 armed guards surrounded the death chamber; as Texas Rangers, National Guards, and other military personnel patrolled the premises, Sankofa's fate rested in the hope that Clarence Thomas would vote in favor of a hearing. After all, he was the one who coined the term, "high-tech lynching." In hindsight, Thomas's vote against Sankofa was certainly not the decisive one, as his mind was undoubtedly made up before any consideration was given.

African American political leadership, on the surface, seemed to support the idea of halting the legal lynching of Shaka Sankofa. This is because unlike in other similar instances, massive support had been mobilized throughout the span of his campaign for a new trial. At the height of his campaign, Sankofa was, in his own perceptive words, a "cause célèbre." Numerous local, national, and international leaders had voiced support, and there was an unprecedented groundswell of grassroots support throughout the Texas area. His leadership, and the movement around him, served as a catalyst for the broader anti-death penalty movement. In the final days leading up to Sankofa's execution, African American (pro-death penalty) Senator Rodney Ellis, for instance, urged the Texas Board of Pardons and Paroles to not only vote on his clemency but to do so publicly as opposed to simply faxing or telephoning in their votes. As Ellis stated in a letter to the board's African American chairman, Gerald Garrett, and obtained by the *Fort Worth Star-Telegram*, "Serious concerns have been raised about the Gary Graham case."[41]

Publicly Ellis expressed concerns about the process, however, as governor for a day he was vested with all the powers of the governor. In fact, because then Governor George W. Bush was campaigning for president, Ellis served as governor for 31 days prior to being elected governor for a day. But during this time he

Employees of the Department of Public Safety stand guard outside the Walls
Unit in Huntsville, Texas where Shaka Sankofa was the 222nd person executed
by the state of Texas since the reinstatement of the death penalty in 1976.
Photo courtesy of L.V. Gaither

remained completely silent, and, up until Sankofa's execution, had
presided over three and halted one. Further commentary on Ellis's
decision, as well as the decisions of numerous other mainstream
African American leaders to posture support for Sankofa, would
be conjectural on my part, but it led me to question their historical relationship to legal lynching. As earlier noted, I was expecting
to meet these African Americans in Gildersleeve's photo.

Chapter Two

All James T. Byrd, Jr. Wanted Was a Ride: Lynching and Police Powers in Texas

> One of the ingredients of the Anglo-Saxon myth is the claim to moral superiority, but black Americans do not share the morality that is expressed in attacking school buses bringing children to a newly integrated school, in dynamiting churches and blowing to bits little black girls, in conducting medical experiments in which blacks suffering from syphilis are deliberately left untreated. Blacks have fought against those who would oppress them, but they have not organized lynch mobs and carved up the flesh of their victims as souvenirs.
>
> —Herbert Shapiro, *White Violence and Black Response*

In small-town America—where everyone knows everybody—it is not uncommon for folks to offer rides to someone heading in the same direction. On June 7, 1998, after attending a family get-together earlier in the evening, forty-nine-year-old "African American male suspect" James T. Byrd began his walk home into the nocturnal hours of the morning along Martin Luther King, Jr. Boulevard, a dark and heavily wooded residential area in East Jasper, Texas. At some point, Byrd was offered his ride from three white males riding east in a pickup truck. One of them he apparently knew and, perhaps, might have considered a friend; we may never know their full relationship. What we do know is that after being beaten and battered nearly to death and having his face "minstrelized" with black spray paint, Byrd was brutalized and sadistically tortured by these men.

Chained by both ankles to the back of the pickup truck, he was dragged for three miles along a winding blacktop road through the woods and finally, after suffering what had to have been indescribable pain, he was murdered. At one point, he was decapitated, and at another, his right arm was ripped apart. Throughout the nightmarish ordeal, other parts of his now-mangled corpse were randomly dismembered—one after the other—so that all one had to do to estimate how far his body had been dragged was to follow the trail of blood and flesh. His killers left parts of his body in front of an African American church. There is no way of imagining how much pain he suffered before his death, but within hours the news had blanketed the national and international media; America as well as other nations once again entered into the ritual of discussing race relations.[1]

Discussing antiblack violence in America too often ends up being a fruitless endeavor, and it is for this reason that I really did not have much to say in response to the news of James T. Byrd's murder. Like millions of others throughout the world, we privately expressed outrage, but further thoughts on ways of expressing our concerns as a community were quickly blurred and distracted by responses from African American political leadership.

In attempting to reflect on Byrd's murder, however, I have appropriated the language of policing and surveillance—in the above narrative the victim is referred to as a suspect—because this adjective "suspicious" expresses the historical and fundamental status of Africans in American society and partly explains American ambivalence toward the question of black victimization. To be sure, Byrd's violent encounter with three white males takes place against the U.S. historical backdrop of state-sponsored and antiblack violence. Alleged/convicted killers Shawn Berry, John William "Bill" King, and Lawrence Brewer, Jr., were not enlisted as "law enforcement" agents, but their brutal behavior fits well within the historical context of antiblack terror not uncommon among law-enforcement officials functioning in manner similar to neo-Nazi militias.

In recent years, reports of police brutality have become routine. Yet most of the corporate-owned media have focused on hate groups such as the Ku Klux Klan or the Aryan Nation. This has largely obscured police brutality and racism within the criminal justice system. By situating antiblack vigilantism and state-sanctioned violence in the same framework, we can better devise strategies that allow us to move one step closer to, without moving two steps backward from, the solution.

On July 12, 1998, six Houston policemen, based on an informant's tip and without a warrant, stormed into the apartment of Chicano/Hispanic American Pedro Oregón and executed him: They shot him twelve times, nine times in the back. In total, police fired over thirty shots; Oregón fired none. Even while no evidence was presented to a grand jury that Oregón had fired at the policemen, as the officers argued initially, all six policemen were acquitted, except for one who was charged with misdemeanor trespassing. (In 1999, two of the officers, Darrel Strouse and James Willis, received federal indictments.) During a rally for Oregón, several Chicano/Hispanic parents stepped forward to give testimony to the deaths of their children at the hands of police. One elderly man, who spoke little English—he spoke through a translator—stated that his son was "handcuffed and suffocated; the police argued that he had suffocated himself with a plastic device while handcuffed facing the ground. He was killed on a Tuesday yet his body was not allowed to be buried by the family; instead the police buried his body on Saturday." Often it is through these types of testimonies, not mainstream news reports, that we learn about the extent of state-sanctioned violence.

Nevertheless, Amnesty International, a relatively mainstream organization, issued a report on police abuse in New York City and Los Angeles, concluding that it had run amok and out of control.[2] A nationwide study of police brutality and accountabil-

ity in the United States by Human Rights Watch, another relatively nonradical entity, drew similar conclusions. It stated that
"Police officers engage in unjustified shootings, severe beatings,
fatal chokings, and unnecessarily rough physical treatment in
cities throughout the United States, while their police superiors,
city officials, and the Justice Department fail to act decisively to
restrain or penalize such acts or even to record the full magnitude of the problem."[3] No more than three months after Byrd's
murder, two firefighters and a policeman in New York City participated in Labor Day Parade float that mocked Byrd's murder.
"Black to the Future" was the name of the float, and while nine
white men wearing Afro and dreadlock wigs threw watermelons
and fried chicken and blasted boom boxes, a mannequin was
dragged in the float's wake, apparently symbolizing Byrd. Such
reports illustrate the fact that policing and surveillance need not
be associated with the state alone, just as mob violence need not
be viewed synonymously with vigilantism.

How do we understand the diverse modalities by which antiblack violence expresses itself in order to perceive it in its entirety,
and how can we be better prepared to mobilize and organize
against it in the twenty-first century? There must be a way to
articulate resistance to antiblack violence without ignoring or
acquiescing to state-sanctioned violence.

What is commonly known of Byrd's death is mostly imagined, conjectures spurred on by the extraordinary media coverage in the United States and abroad. Fueling media perceptions,
in the aftermath of Byrd's murder, people, mostly politicians, said
whatever came into their heads. According to the Reverend Jesse
Jackson, Sr., "Byrd's death so shocked the country that it has caused
all Americans to think about the ills of hate and racism[and]...
could very well change the state of the nation." NAACP Executive Director Kweisi Mfume commented, "[T]hese cowards
should never walk the street again as free men"; and the Reverend
Al Sharpton stated, "As Brother Byrd's body was torn, America's
spirit was torn, and we need to reweave it with equal protection

under the law." Although these types of pronouncements coming from public leaders dominate in political rhetoric, they sharply contradict the reality of Americans' attitudes toward race: Most white Americans, polls tell us, believe that racism is not a major problem in the United States. Furthermore, based on this type of rhetoric, this atrocity appears to be an aberration. In addition, they obscure the nature of antiblack vigilantism, which often stems from police measures and fosters the assumption that corrections officers can honestly police themselves. Are we to believe that as pogroms against "nonwhite" peoples escalate, popular empathy will sway in the direction of black victimization, or that harsher and lengthier prison terms will counterbalance antiblack violence? Such comments regarding the murder of James Byrd may have been voiced without much thought; perhaps they even were overlooked by most who heard or read them; nevertheless, they also underscored the inability, and perhaps even unwillingness, of African American leaders to come up with effective strategies for mobilizing resistance to antiblack and state violence. Their blind and narrow predisposition toward the state in thinking of ways to resolve antiblack vigilantism is indeed disquieting.

RACIAL POLICING

It has become fashionable for the dominant media to focus attention on the polarization in attitudes among white and black Americans regarding racism. The majority white population is unaware of (or collectively shares a different reality from) the African American experience of policing; for blacks, police brutality is an everyday reality, given the routine stops and illegal automobile searches by police; for suburban whites, secure and safely isolated from blacks and Latinos, such policing is rare and unfamiliar.

Of course, whites do not have the historical experience of being hunted by vigilantes enforcing white supremacy. With the popularity of television shows like *N.Y. Undercover*, *Law and Order*, *L.A. Law*, *Cops*, and *America's Most Wanted*, to name just a few, it is inconceivable that any significant portion of the white population is unaware of black victimization. The question is: How do whites view black victimization?

On one hand, the menacing specter of privatized prison construction and militarization of the nation's police forces reflect the public's growing anxiety, which stems from routine news reporting on crime and violence, and their insecurities in an uncertain economy.[4] On the other hand, it reflects the inability or unwillingness of those representatives whose constituencies would stand to gain from the eradication of the death penalty and the demilitarization and downsizing of the criminal justice system to develop radical critiques of the criminal justice system. Because no new solutions have been offered, the public views black victimization through an ahistorical and highly racialized prism.

RACIAL POLICING AND VIGILANTISM

In hopes of counteracting the escalation of violent criminal activities that run the gamut from social crimes, through hate crimes, to police brutality, civil rights leaders and other black representatives (out of desperation or belief in the rhetoric of "victims rights" groups funded by right-wing philanthropy) call upon the very same state apparatuses that historically have been the most ardent repressors of the political struggles of blacks to police their own communities (The works of writers Ward Churchill, Jim Vander Wall, and Kenneth O'Reilly all document this fact.).[5] Of course, it is essential to comprehend the historical relationship between legal violence and extralegal vigilante violence against blacks in the United States to gain a deeper understanding of what appears to be a resurgence of police brutality and antiblack vigilantism.

State-approved and antiblack vigilantism historically developed hand in hand, beginning in the early period of colonial America. Slave patrols (also known as "patterollers") emerged at the beginning of the eighteenth century, setting the pattern of policing that people of African descent would experience throughout America. W. Marvin Dulaney, director of the Avery Research Center for African American History at the College of Charleston, describes in *Black Police in America* the development of his policing:

> By the middle of the eighteenth century, every southern colony had a slave patrol. Although in some communities all white males were required to serve some time as patterollers, their ranks were usually filled with poor whites. The patrols were authorized to stop, search, whip, maim, and even kill any African slave caught off the plantation without a pass, engaged in illegal activities, or running away. The patterollers policed specific geographic areas in southern communities called "beats." Paramilitary in nature, the slave patrol often cooperated with the militia in the southern colonies to prevent and suppress slave insurrections. To facilitate the rapid mobilization of the patrol and to ensure that every white man supported its activities in emergencies, colonial governments granted all whites the authority to detain, whip, and even kill slaves suspected of illegal activities or conspiracies. The colonial slave patrol exercised awesome powers which were often abused.[6]

The mandate to police blacks through both the criminal justice system and vigilantism carried over into the nineteenth century, after slavery had been abolished, and later still, into the era of Reconstruction that was dismantled by the southern ruling planter class.[7] Civil War historian William Friedheim's *Freedom's Unfinished Revolution* outlines the shape of post-Reconstruction racism:

> Denied land, African Americans became economically dependent, politically disenfranchised, socially segregated, and routinely targeted for acts of chilling and often officially approved violence. From 1890 to 1900, an average of 175 African Americans were lynched each year, many burned or dismembered beyond identification. Public officials in the South did not condemn lynching and did not punish those responsible. By their

silence and inaction, but more often by highly visible
and vocal encouragements, southern politicians and
government leaders endorsed racial violence.[8]

Between 1888 and 1918, a black man was lynched every two
or three days. In some cases, thousands of white citizens and law-
enforcement officers gathered to cheer on the perpetrators. Perpetrators were virtually always listed as "unknown" and hardly
ever prosecuted by the criminal justice system. Jerome G. Miller,
president of the National Center on Institutions and Alternatives, wrote in his book *Search and Destroy*:

> In the "informal" justice system in the United States,
> the most extreme punishments and unjust proce-
> dures for blacks were never beyond tacit support of a
> substantial proportion of the white population well
> into this century. Castration, lynching, and other
> vigilante-type actions were characteristically reserved
> for citizens of color and provided the backdrop and
> collective memory against which the formal criminal
> justice system functioned when it came to blacks.[9]

Given American history, the murder of James T. Byrd
was as shocking to some as it was predictable to others. There
are those who stood aghast at the news of Byrd's murder; who
felt, or rather hoped, that race relations had improved beyond
such acts of terror and murder. Others, however, knowing the
anxiety surrounding the possibilities of widespread, violent racial
strife understood the historical context for what was reportedly
shouted by one of Byrd's assailants: "We're going to start 'The
Turner Diaries' early! *The Turner Diaries*,[10] written by the late
university professor William Pierce (under the *nom de plume*
Andrew McDonald), has become a widely circulated handbook
for thousands of antigovernment, white militia groups.

The Reverend Jackson was right: Byrd's killing sent signals beyond
the confines of Texas, affecting the already racially charged climate
of American society. But he was right for the wrong reasons.

HATE CRIMES

As noted by the Southern Poverty Law Center's Winter 1999 *Intelligence Report*, Byrd's murder did not occur in a vacuum. Racially motivated crimes committed in the months prior to Byrd's slaying include Robert J. Neville, Jr. and Michael W. Hall's February abduction and shooting of Amy Robinson in Fort Worth, Texas.

Mistaking Robinson, who was white but with dark black hair, for an African American, the men used her for target practice (both Neville and Hall were convicted of murder in separate trials). Little more than a week after Byrd's murder, similar acts of violence against blacks were reported in newspapers across the country. One example was the case of Baron Manning of Belleville, Illinois, a town near East St. Louis. An act of mock violence similar to the brutal death of Byrd was carried out against the seventeen-year-old Manning, but the local police department, local prosecutors, and national media declared it to be a botched drug deal.[11]

In attempting to construct a rational explanation for the violence committed against Byrd, we also must consider at the same time both the sociopolitical context in which the murder occurred and the experiences and perspectives of those who committed the violent act. Each of the alleged killers was a poverty-stricken veteran of the Texas Department of Corrections (which suggests all had suffered their own kind of victimization and the historical antagonisms between poor whites and blacks).

Why did these men harbor such antiblack white rage? Had the perpetrators been of a more privileged economic class, would they have been treated in the same manner? Would there have been such a rush to judgment by the media and society? Would the public even have heard about the event? Would all of the defendants receive the death penalty if convicted for Byrd's death? How do we who are adamantly opposed to the death penalty maintain such a position in cases like Jasper? A whole medley of issues—hate crime, death penalty, and those of race and class—converged in Jasper, Texas, on June 9, 1998.

America has a long way to go to standardize its definition of "hate crimes." While in 1992 Congress enacted legislation that required police departments throughout the country to make regular reports on crimes believed to fall under the Uniform Crime Reports' definition of "hate crimes," no more than a quarter of the law-enforcement agencies have participated in the project. Despite official recognition of various types of hate-crime legislation, police agencies throughout the country continue to express uncertainty over how to define hate crimes and appear hesitant to participate fully in the project. U.S. Civil Rights Commission Chair Mary Frances Berry writes in *Black Resistance, White Law*: "Police departments expressed continuing dismay about... when to categorize an assault as a hate crime or simply as an assault."[12]

However, more hate crimes are committed against African Americans (in proportion to their population) than against any other ethnic group. Overall, in 1997 there were 331 incidents of reported hate crimes, and African Americans ranked highest as victims, followed by gays and lesbians and Latino Americans respectively. As Byrd's death clearly demonstrated, the state of Texas shares in this country's legacy of racial violence. But what hand does the government have in adding fuel to the fire?

The *Uniform Crime Reports (UCR)* provide the most widely cited statistics on hate crime in the United States. Over the past two decades the rates of robbery, rape, and aggravated assault, according to *UCR* statistics, increased dramatically. These reports greatly influenced the public's perception of violent crime as being completely out of control and provided the rationale for increased repression and policies to get tougher on "criminals." Berry notes that

> Years of unimpeded, festering racism encouraged racially motivated violence against blacks and police abuse unavenged and unpunished. The justice system,

even in cities with black mayors, remained largely unresponsive to the problems of police abuse. The Justice Department's response to police abuse and racially motivated violence during the Carter administration slightly improved over the record of preceding years, but retreat became the byword in the Reagan-Bush years. The Klan, skinheads, and other organizations received attention but not the police abuse or individual intimidation shown to African-Americans seeking housing or education. The result during the Reagan-Bush years was increased racial polarization, hate crimes, and reports of police brutality.[13]

STATE CRIMES: THE DEATH PENALTY IN TEXAS

In 1998 Governor George W. Bush broke a long tradition in Texas of not providing clemency, doing so for Henry Lee Lucas, a convicted serial killer. And there was the spectacle and public outrage around pickax murderer Karla Faye Tucker's execution, which saw reactionary demagogue Pat Robertson joining together with Pope John Paul II to protest. But with few exceptions, state executions occur regularly in Huntsville, Texas, and are met with little organized protest or state intervention. Racism apparent in death penalty statistics for Texas also encounters little opposition.

Outcomes based on race in death penalty cases have a long history in Texas. Historically, the defendant's race played a large role in determining who was executed in the state. Between 1924 and 1972, 361 people were put to death in Texas; 70 percent of them were "nonwhite"; blacks constituted 63 percent of those killed. This statistic reflects the postbellum years in Texas where most—nearly all—lynching victims were black.[14]

Today the state of Texas is responsible for a third of the executions in the United States. If every state had copied Texas in 1993 alone, there would have been 250 executions, one for every business day of the year. In 1997, thirty-seven prisoners were executed in Huntsville. Accordingly, blacks are represented on death row at three and a half times their proportion in the population as a whole.

As many had hoped, the murderers of James T. Byrd were convicted, two of them to death. It was the first time in the history of Texas, and one of the few times in the history of the United States, white offenders were sentenced to death for the murder of a black person.

EVADING RACE AND RESPONSIBILITY

When Camille Cosby, wife of entertainer Bill Cosby, made national headlines by suggesting that racism in America provided the context for Russian immigrant Mikail Markhasev's socialization and so was partly responsible for her son's murder, she was accused of condemning all whites and American society in general for the behavior of one individual. "An unfair judgment," many argued. But Cosby's commentary was as instructive as the response it invoked. Nevertheless, the politics of evasion invariably accompany antiblack violence and the response to Cosby was in no way unusual. First, there is the denial and/or obfuscation of the historical context within which the violence occurs. Just as there are those who deny that the Holocaust against Jews, Roma, gays/lesbians, and political dissidents occurred in Germany's Third Reich, there are those today who deny the level of European involvement in the transatlantic slave trade, which resulted in the underdevelopment of the African continent, genocide, and centuries of chattel enslavement of Africans in America.

Elected officials denounced Byrd's killing. A U.S. House of Representatives' resolution, which extended condolences to Byrd's family, was unanimously passed on a 397 to 0 vote. But why should a representative from outside the East Texas district initiate the resolution of condemnation? Texas Representative Sheila Jackson-Lee (D-Houston) introduced the House resolution, not Jim Turner (D-Crockett), in whose district the murder occurred.[15] Turner, who supported the resolution, echoed Martin Luther King, Jr.'s vision that every American be judged not by the color of their skin but by the content of their character, stating "No American is safe until every American treats his neighbor with dignity, regardless of the color of his skin."[16] But Turner failed to specify whom he was talking about, obfuscating racial injustices against blacks.

Another type of evasion occurs in the form of distancing from the crime; downplaying and/or obscuring the climate and legacy of racism that fuels the current antiblack violent behavior. For instance, Jasper's Sheriff Billy Rowles was quoted in the *Houston Chronicle* as saying that "every law enforcement agency within 200 miles has offered to help in the investigation...[and that most] of his 14 deputies... had to handle routine law enforcement calls during their days off because they[were] so busy with the Byrd investigation."[17] But despite the nature of the crime, the fact that East Texas is widely known to be a focal point for Klan-related activities, that the murderers' bodies were tattooed with white supremacist images, that they had been investigated by the Texas Department of Corrections for alleged ties to the Ku Klux Klan, and even despite the sheriff's acknowledgement that they may have had connections with white supremacy groups, Rowles seemed anxious to rule out the racism. As the white sheriff put it, amid hisses and bursts of laughter from African Americans living in Jasper who attended the national press conference, "We have no organized KKK or Aryan Brotherhood groups here in Jasper County."[18]

CONCLUSION

Historically, from the era of slavery to the present, a variety of tactics and strategies have been employed by blacks to protect themselves from antiblack violence. Oftentimes, particularly during the post-civil rights movement, the strategies and tactics have been formulated in response to incidents similar to the atrocity in Jasper, or the Rodney King beating, which sparked a pseudorebellion in Los Angeles and other cities across the United States. Indeed, responses have ranged from armed revolts, to nonviolent protest, to subservient accommodation.[19] But on rare occasions, particularly since the passage of the Civil Rights Act of 1965, the media have projected black responses to violence outside the confines of accomodationism.

Byrd's murder evoked, at least in style if not in substance, these three historical forms of response to white antiblack violence, forms that indicate that African Americans, as a whole, remain uncertain and ambiguous about their political and social status, and for good reason—our status has been and continues to be questionable. There were calls for love, healing, and reconciliation; there were calls for arming the community for self-defense; and finally, there was the call for calm—to let the state and federal authorities handle it. What was conspicuously absent, however, was a radical response that placed the incident in its historical and current political context, that revealed the partnership among racist policing, state executions and racist violence. African Americans must resolve this ambiguity regarding the question of racial repression in order to create the necessary weapons to address reactionary forms of criminalization and the apparent resurgence of antiblack violence.

Major political and structural changes are needed to address police brutality, the racist application of the death penalty, and the mass incarceration of blacks; such changes also must address vigilantism. These political and structural changes will not come about through humdrum race advisory boards and town hall meetings such as those initiated and managed by President Clinton's "Presidential Race Initiative." In fact, the establishment media will never even entertain such ideas unless there is organized resistance centered on a clear ideological threat to the existing economic, political, and social hegemony.

Chapter Three

African American Leadership Responses to the Increasing Significance of Whiteness

What, to the American slave, is your 4th of July?

—Frederick Douglass

Blacks must accept the reality that for the white race, democracy and racial oppression are not conflicting ideals.

—Dr. Mario Beatty

In 1852 Frederick Douglass was invited by the Rochester Ladies Anti Slavery Society to deliver an oration at an event commemorating the Fourth of July. At the time Rochester, New York was considered by many to be an epicenter of antislavery activities, thus any opportunity to speak before such an audience would undoubtedly serve the cause of abolition. But Douglass— perhaps as a rhetorical pretext, perhaps solely out of principle— agreed to speak only if the event was held the following day, July 5. The organizers of the event apparently agreed, and after the capacity crowd of nearly 600 people had assembled inside Corinthian Hall, Douglass proceeded to deliver what many consider to be one of the most celebrated antislavery orations ever given.[1] In it he questioned the very foundations of national mythology by then firmly fixed in America's collective consciousness; he referred to the holiday as "your national independence"; and his feelings about the principles of "freedom" and "liberty" were reflected in the manner he delivered the words I've chosen as the primary epigraph for this chapter.[2]

Although Douglass's speech appears to contradict any semblance of patriotic sensibility, its oppositional tone toward American empire resonates clearly within the liberal lingua franca of today. That the speech was acutely indicative of the temperament of his time makes its timelessness all the more resoundingly ironic in a society that eventually abolished chattel slavery, enacted civil rights laws, and today boasts of being a multiracial democracy.

Douglass, to be sure, probably could have used any of the popular holidays to issue his reproach, for holidays play a vital role in the construction of national narratives. Originally referred to as "holy days" and set aside by the powers that be as religious festivals where no work was done, in modern times they symbolize histories collectively perceived as sacred and significant, revealing the value society places on the contributions of particular groups and individuals in a nation's cultural development. It is here that the sense of collective identity is strengthened.

Such holidays as St. Patrick's Day and Yom Kippur—among many others—remind us of the diversity and multicultural heritage of America. For the culturally literate, St. Patrick's Day might very well conjure up images of the fighting Irish and green beer. During Yom Kippur, we envision Jews abstaining from drink, food, and sexual intercourse, not putting on leather shoes, and anointing themselves with oil. Such holidays reinforce the commonly held belief that America is a melting pot, inclusive of all the diverse ethnic groups that have contributed to its development. When St. Patrick's Day arrives, it isn't at all unusual to witness Asians, African Americans, and other non-Irish people taking part in the celebrations just as enthusiastically as the Irish themselves.[3] Aren't these individuals saying, in essence, they accept the other group? Or rather, and perhaps more appropriate for this analysis, are they themselves expressing their desire to be accepted?

Of course, enlisting holidays is just one aspect of narrating nationhood. Film, electronic media, literature, religion, language, sports, and architecture all serve to signify presence and acceptance as well. Taken as a whole, these genres of cultural representation constitute a "master narrative"[4] that maintains age-old assumptions regarding America's history and national identity. At face value, particularly among individuals possessing an ahistorical consciousness, the themes imparted in this narrative conjecture the appearance of a shared cultural experience regardless of sex, race, class, religion, sexual orientation, and such. But upon more careful consideration, one will discover or recognize its significance to the overall construction, maintenance, and constant revision of whiteness. Douglass was in unequivocal terms suggesting that Africans were not privileged agents of this grand narrative of human enlightenment called America.

The persistent issue of whiteness is what Douglass was ultimately responding to, as he asked his audience to self-reflect on their idle privilege. The set of ideas and social practices that attempt to universalize whiteness while particularizing otherness often functions less visibly than overt racism, but the part it plays in maintaining a status quo of inequality and oppression based primarily around "race" is unquestionable. Douglass's audience was comprised mostly of white individuals who perhaps probably didn't identify themselves, or the abolition movement, as anti-African, yet failed short in critically engaging their own personal prejudices regarding race and place in American society. Although perhaps opposed to human slavery in the South, they hardly conceived of a postslavery society where Africans would be granted full citizenship rights and structures designed to circumscribe their progress would be completely abolished. Instead, from the very beginning of the construction of the present racial hierarchy, Africans were clearly assigned to the bottom; first as slaves, second as denizens, then as superfluous labor, and finally as peripheral subjects to the social, political, and economic order.

This global system has remained intact for more than a century after his speech.

Douglass's speech occurred within a context. The carefully scripted "Fifth of July" speech, as it came to be known, was a unique and dynamic self-assertion of his growing independence from the paternalism of the white-male-dominated sector of the antislavery movement. Within months of the speech Douglass had severed all organizational ties with his fellow abolitionists, most notably William Lloyd Garrison, Wendell Phillips, and Edmund Quincy. The rift between these important individuals revolved around politics, interpretations of the Constitution, and Douglass's own personal career development—so we are told.

William S. McFeely, in his biography *Frederick Douglass* suggests that the "Garrisonians, despite their official secularism, regarded any deviation from their leadership as heresy: theirs was the only way; all others were wrong."[5] Indeed, Garrison and his followers had a reputation of being steadfast and determined, albeit strongly sectarian, in their uncompromising pursuit of justice. They shunned political action and, instead, favored moral suasion; they favored disunion, and viewed the Constitution as inherently evil. Douglass, a self-assured figure in his own right, would eventually break from the Garrisonian mold in favor of combining political action with moral suasion, and after much discussion with the towering antislavery politician Gerrit Smith, he began to speak of the Constitution as a document unfavorable to slavery. It is safe to suggest that the rift between Douglass and the Garrisonians revolved primarily around political strategies and outlook. But to do so might very well blind one to the ways in race and ideology have interacted in modern history.

In his biographical account of William Lloyd Garrison, *All On Fire*, Henry Mayer suggests that while it is tempting, it would be, "dangerous, to discern a racial dimension in the conflict and regard the abolitionist establishment as endeavoring to keep Douglass 'in his place.'"[6] Yet beneath the veneer of ideological divergence, the color line was as visible then as it is in Mayer's attempt to gloss over it today. I would share in the opinion that Garrison's behavior and attitude toward blacks was perhaps as progressive then as among even the most visible black leaders today, and was certainly centuries further along than the general white public of his time.

Nevertheless, throughout McFeely's biography of Douglass it is repeatedly revealed how at nearly every turn in his life and career as an abolitionist, Douglass was confronted with the racial prejudice and paternalism of his fellow abolitionists—including Garrison—with the two more often than not converging, making it tempting for historians to dismiss the former for the latter.

Eventually, as Douglass increasingly interacted with fellow black abolitionists such as Henry Highland Garnet and Martin R. Delaney and became more directly involved in the Negro convention movement, the necessity of racial consciousness and solidarity began to illuminate more clearly for him. Toward the end of his career as an abolitionist, Douglass came to the conclusion that blacks must be in control of their own advocacy and representation within in the context of a broader, multiracial movement. Douglass's life stood at the center of most of the important events of the nineteenth century regarding black America's struggle for freedom. Looking back, his career as an abolitionist proves increasingly instructive to a new generation of activists in the twenty-first century, even as the landscape for social change in America has changed considerably.

WHITE NATIONALISM AND SLAVERY

In the United States master narratives have historically served the purpose of fostering nationalist values and enforcing a highly racialized concept of citizenship, signaling and legitimating whiteness by virtue of the manner in which otherness (blackness) has been constructed. White nationalism has historically extended across the entire ideological, social, and class range of American society. That is, by the time the government of the United States was formed in 1776, white nationalism had already seized the collective consciousness of American citizens. The white-led abolitionist movement, which eventually played a major part in the abolition of chattel slavery (but not the dominant role), was not at all immune from racial prejudice, and this was the principal reason for its limited success. Finally, the ideology of white supremacy, and the lack of ideological response to it, continues to be the principal barrier to achieving multiracial political cooperation.

Such an argument in today's reactionary climate could easily be dismissed as racial paranoia, even among blacks themselves; or perhaps trivial nit-picking identity politics in some circles. But if understood in historical and social context, the pervasiveness of whiteness becomes transparent, and the seriousness of this recurring problem warrants immediate attention, as new generations of activists are compelled by history to take on the burden of an enduring, protracted, and unfinished struggle for freedom. Underlying this vision of freedom has been a continued struggle against an insistent denial of citizenship on the part of the powers that be, a denial of some of the most fundamental human rights known in the modern period of human history. And even though the dominant society has historically resisted such efforts at social change, every small gain has impacted the broader social landscape in ways that have expanded the concept of democracy.

Master narratives have dominated our view of the world, our collective sense of the past, present, and future. A century and a half has passed since Douglass's speech, yet millions of Americans, including the newly arrived, immerse themselves in patriotic gaiety on the date the Declaration of Independence was adopted in 1776. Such acts of "patriotism" appear reasonable enough. After all, citizenship in the United States does have its privileges, and this is readily apparent to a newly arrived immigrant from the war-torn region of southern Mexico (Chiapas), even if they're struggling to survive, working two to three bare-minimum-wage jobs, or perhaps a second-generation Cambodian professional whose parents escaped the holocaust conditions of the Khmer Rogue by boat across the Pacific Ocean; but because of their parents' hard work and sacrifice, they have succeeded. Historically, America's shores have represented freedom and liberty from afar, and more than a few have realized their dreams. But for the children of the enslaved Africans, the Atlantic was, and continues to be, an eerie and ghostly "Middle Passage"; an ongoing nightmare, only to be halted by a collective journey toward "Social Death."[7] Our arrival to the Americas signaled death, both in physical, spiritual, and social terms.

According to historian Orlando Patterson, slavery is "The permanent, violent domination of natally alienated and generally dishonored persons." No doubt, others have defined slavery differently, but despite this widespread indistinctness we witness among scholars, most radical historians will agree that what distinguishes New World slavery from other historical forms is its permanency; that even in its aftermath it merely undergoes transmutations. Robin Blackburn warns of excessively blurring the lines between the slavery of the New World and that of the Ancient and medieval world.

> In other societies slavery has had a chameleon-like ability to adapt to the surrounding social formation; like a social false limb it has extended the powers of slaveholders in forms appropriate to the given society—perhaps enlarging a lineage or supplying a trusted core of administrators. In the eighteenth century Americas the use of slaves in agriculture and mining helped to extend the scope of mercantile and manufacturing capital and supplied industrializing regions with needed inputs and outlets.[8]

Thus, New World slavery was distinctively cruel, coercive, continuous, and intensely physical. The sole purpose of this form of slavery was to make Africans a commoditized property.

During the reign of the Ottoman Empire, for example, European Christian subjects were required every few years to levy some of their adolescent males to the empire as a form of taxation. Through this collecting system known as the *devshirme*, these children were taken from their families and trained for service in the Ottoman government. The majority of them were eventually enrolled in the Janissary corps, a military infantry equipped with more firepower than any other military force in the world at the time. The Janissary corps was essentially a slave army, forbidden from trading, confined to barracks, and not allowed to marry. These slaves, however, eventually became a powerful force within the Ottoman Empire, and by the eighteenth century they were no longer a disciplined slave army confined to fighting the wars of the Ottoman Empire; they had over a period of time gained special privileges, were marrying, and engaging in lucrative trade.[9] This was not to be the case with the formerly enslaved Africans in the New World.

Some have argued—and this perhaps is the most popular view—that the Atlantic slave trade was not necessarily harmful to the African continent or those forcibly transported to the new world because Africans themselves practiced slavery, thus, the Middle Passage was simply a logical outgrowth of European progress. Several serious scholars—from Walter Rodney to Boubacar Barry—have set the record straight with their balanced perspectives.[10] If the reader relies on historians (i.e., Philip Curtin[11]) to contextualize their historical sense of the impact that slavery had on Africans as a race, then it is possible that little of the following will make much sense.

Had the government at the end of the Civil War developed a system of reparations for the ex-slaves, New World slavery might possibly be looked upon by historians as just one of the numerous instances of slavery. Far less tragic narratives like "Up from Slavery" and "From Slavery to Freedom"[12] could then have been accurately projected into the public's consciousness by historians. But such provisions never occurred, thus, slavery has been a door of no return. America is truly a nation of immigrants, but African Americans did not immigrate to these shores. The unacknowledged legacy of slavery has much to do with the ignorance of its impact upon the present, and has much to do with the increasing pervasiveness of whiteness in American empire.

THE AMERICAN REVOLUTION PERIOD

Early on we are taught to believe the American Revolution was a watershed event in modern human history, but the ideals accompanying the Revolution took shape in a historical context inundated with moral inconsistencies, setting in motion many of the social and political contradictions prevalent in America today. Sure, the demands for freedom and self-determination made by the colonists against the metropolitan officials and merchants were incongruent with the reality of them holding Africans in chattel bondage. However, despite these historical contradictions that impact strongly on the present, the ruling class in America has been able to maintain anglocentric hegemony among most of its citizens, including those of color and blacks.

For instance, African Americans celebrate Independence Day as if liberty and equality for the founding fathers was somehow tied to freedom for their enslaved ancestors and, as I've already noted, this day gives the impression of a shared historical experience, even among the poorest of the poor. However, appearances can be deceiving. And they can be disturbing to those who harbor differences of perspective. Despite the incessant incantations of imperialist and settler historians, the independence won from the British homeland in 1776 did not result in the withering away of a white supremacy ideology, nor was that the point of it. The phrase, "All men are created equal," eventually came to this: White-skinned American men were equal to their former British colonial masters. The vast majority of white Americans conceived of liberty and freedom in political and economic terms, and in nationalist terms that excluded the enslaved Africans. In fact, as the thirteen colonies gained their independence from the British homeland, it was an early forewarning of the type of "rhetorical ethic"[13] that would come to characterize moral discourse in Western society.

A common mistake by historians is to ignore inconsistent patterns of verbal iconography within the dominant European culture. In her book *Yurugu: An African-centered Critique of European Cultural Thought and Behavior*, Marimba Ani argues that within European culture, there exists a statement of moral behavior, a rhetorical ethic, which has no meaning for the members of that culture. Thus, when historians refer to the ideals embedded within the Declaration of Independence as being universally applied, they sometimes make the mistake of assuming the founding fathers had certain egalitarian ideals that they didn't live up to rather than understanding the propagation of certain values as rhetoric, nothing more or less. In fact, the notion of black inferiority was not, as John S. Haller, Jr. put it, simply "the solipsistic invention of a few; rather it was the mythology of a nation."[14]

The growing popularization of the natural-rights ideology considerably changed Anglo American outlooks toward slavery. According to Merton L. Dillon, in his book *Slavery Attacked*, "White colonists long had viewed the growing black population with misgiving. Now, with increasing concern for the welfare of individuals and for the proper limits of power, whites began to doubt the justice of their actions and to question even the moral basis of their society."[15] There is little doubt the moral contradiction of slavery seemed apparent to some of the colonists, and there were in fact increasing political and philosophical challenges to the peculiar institution during this time. Nevertheless, even though numerous Africans joined hands with their plantation masters to fight the British—in many instances standing proxy for them—their fate would be remarkably different from that of their white comrades. The system of slavery was maintained by the majority of Anglo-Americans who themselves spoke endlessly of liberty and equality.

Africans fought from beginning to end; from King Street, to Lexington, to Concord, Africans fought. Yet, after the war's conclusion, slavery continued, and although it is worth noting that a far more significant number of Africans realized at the time that their interests weighed more heavily toward a British victory, this African presence in the U.S. military—a recurring fact—is an important point to take note of.[16]

In all fairness, as the war ended some Africans, it could be argued, did gain some forms of freedom, as they escaped with Loyalists and British forces to the colonies of Florida, Jamaica, and Nova Scotia. Others were gradually emancipated for a variety of reasons such as laws, postwar economic factors, and again, the war itself. However, in order to "forestall such circumventions of state emancipation provisions, laws were instituted" so that although numerous Africans were said to be free, they had no legal rights or property to exercise such freedom.[17] Although the spirit of the times gave to them the hope of liberty, it essentially meant the lure of freedom for Anglo Americans and the assurance of perpetual servitude and bondage for the Africans. A racist ideology soundly negating the humanity of Africans was firmly established within a legal framework, prisons and penal colonies were established, and "white men" immediately turned their attention toward westward expansion; in other words, reextermination of the "savage red man."[18]

Colin G. Galloway, in his book *The American Revolution in Indian Country*, points out the following:

> In the end, white America excluded Indians from the republican society the Revolution created. Despite their absence from much of the historical literature, Indian people were everywhere in colonial America. In 1775, Indian nations despite intrusive and disruptive pressures unleashed by European contact still controlled most of America west of the Appalachians. In 1783, when Britain transferred that territory to the new United States, most of it was still

> in Indian hands, but a new era had begun; . . . the
> Revolution elevated acquisition of Indian lands into
> a national policy. The new nation, born of a bloody
> revolution and committed to expansion, could not
> tolerate America as Indian country. Increasingly,
> Americans viewed the future as one without Indians.
> The Revolution both created a new society and pro-
> vided justification for excluding Indians from it.[19]

Generally speaking, the Native American population fared worse than their African counterparts. Their role in this national mythology—their characterization in this historic theatre of conflict—has either been excluded or gravely misrepresented. In popular imagination, their collective misfortune following the war is seen as a consequence of siding with the British and losing; when, in fact, Natives Americans like Africans fought on both sides, and their struggles were informed by their various quests for freedom. At worst they were conceived of as heathens who needed to be simply exterminated or *civilized*.

I see no need to intellectualize the question of who fared better or worse, because what happened to the Native American and African populations are part of the same narrative. Focusing attention on antiblack racism should never be done in a way that reduces the impact or significance of the physical, cultural, and spiritual genocide of indigenous peoples, whether at the inception of Spain's colonization of the Americas, leading up to the period immediately after the Civil War, or well into the colonial present. No discourse on contemporary problems regarding race and place should be constructed in an ahistorical fashion, for doing so contradicts the manner in which historical visions of the world compete with one another in present political discourse.

CONTESTING WHITENESS

Contests over "memories and spaces" have been a recurring problem shaping modern American social relations, but they allow us to gauge, with some degree of accuracy, human progress or lack thereof. Others have proscribed historical memories and spaces accepted as sacred to some because of the horror they invoke, as for example in the southern region of the United States, where black and white citizens have waged fierce debates over the legitimacy of Confederate monuments and flags. For the sons and daughters of the Confederacy, these symbols represent their heritage and the sacredness of their cause; for the sons and daughters of enslaved Africans, they evoke horrific memories of brutality and enslavement.

In Houston, Texas, a "postindustrial city *par excellence*" because of an economy built around advanced technologies (i.e., Enron), Confederate statues, street signs, and buildings loom large upon the landscape as historical reminders, or perhaps as authentication of the survival of white supremacy. Several educational institutions are named for Confederate officials, and it is difficult to meet history teachers who do not instruct their students from a Confederate perspective when discussing the Civil War and slavery. Amid ritzy lofts, phallic-like skyscrapers, and postmodern constructions designed by the likes of architect Robert A.M. Stern stand well-groomed "Hanging Oaks"; one does not sense or feel the demise of Jim Crow even as one strolls through this futuristic city that increasingly resembles the past. The State of Texas represents the tip of the iceberg in regard to such romantic pageantry. Mississippi, Alabama, Louisiana, Georgia, South Carolina, and others present a more vivid picture. It is my belief that these symbols exist in their varied forms for no other reason than the complete unwillingness of those in power to engage the question of their illegitimacy. Indeed, nation-states require historical narratives that its citizens adhere to.

In *Culture and Imperialism*, the late Edward Said argued that although imperialism means taking land away from the indigenous inhabitants, narrative was an important component of its overall weaponry against the oppressed: "The power to narrate, or to block other narratives from forming and emerging, is very important to culture and imperialism, and constitutes one of the main connections between them."[20] Much, if not all, New World history has been shaped by this imperialist logic. And yet, imperialism invariably invokes resistance, and since it is my premise that absent resistance systems of oppression will remain intact, the question becomes not whether there should be resistance but by what means should it be expressed?

Although not necessarily a historical law, movements of resistance have mostly been accompanied by their own alternative beliefs and visions, usually underscored by their own unique symbols (both immediate and historical). "We must canonize our own saints, create our own martyrs, and elevate to positions of fame and honor black men and women who have made their distinct contributions to our racial history,"[21] argued Marcus Garvey (1887-1940), founder of the Universal Negro Improvement Association (UNIA). Garvey would eventually lead one of the largest and most effective mass movements of resistance in the Western hemisphere, and his influence reached across the Atlantic, shaping the outlook of many independence and decolonization movements, and even touching the life of Ho Chi Minh[22] of Vietnam, who on his trips to New York would attend UNIA meetings and take in their vibrant parades that regularly passed through the streets of Harlem.

Garvey was not the first leader to craft an ideology tied in with iconoclastic symbolism as a means to further nationalist movement—Martin Robeson Delaney, Alexander Crummell, Edward Wilmot Blyden, just to name three perhaps lesser-known black nationalist thinkers, each in different ways helped to lay the philosophical and political groundwork for Garvey's black modernist project.[23] Nor would he be the last to apply the concept of nationhood in practical terms. As Molefi Asante notes in his book *Afrocentricity*, Elijah Muhammad's version of Islam was an important moment in the history of black struggle because, "he liberated the symbols of religion, denouncing those that had enslaved us, and provided different, more vital symbols for the African American."[24] And, of course, there was the Black Panther

Party[25] that came on the heels of the civil rights and black power movements.

Those attempting to create and inform cultures of resistance, even in the context of late capitalism, must fully understand the value of reconstructing alternative symbols of resistance to counteract the pervasive and hegemonic symbols of white supremacy. It is not by chance that at this writing, young school children are still taught that in 1492 Christopher Columbus sailed the ocean blue, discovering America; even though China, under the leadership of Emperor Zhu Di, set sail for the New World as early as 1421 in ships whose rudders alone were, according to Gavin Menzies, "almost as long as the whole of the flagship the Niña in which Columbus was later to set sail for the New World."[26] There is a reason why students continue to graduate from high schools and colleges having little or know knowledge of Abu Bakari II, the king of Mali, who sent 200 canoes westward with orders not to return until they reached the ocean's limits[27] in 1312.

Students are taught that Greek civilization originated with Aryans, but, according to Martin Bernal, author of *Black Athena: The Afroasiatic Roots of Classical Civilization*, classical Greeks knew nothing of the popularly used "Aryan Model," but rather subscribed to the "Ancient Model," which held that they were a people essentially civilized through colonization by the Egyptians and Phoenicians. According to Bernal, because of racism, the Afroasiatic roots of classical civilization have been suppressed by European scholars. If Bernal is correct, then the whole basis of Europe's claim to being the harbinger of civilization is not only unfounded, it is deeply fabricated. But historical truth is not the intention of those responsible for perpetuating Eurocentric myths.

No matter how groups construct their vision(s) of freedom or ideology, it must be carefully done with the clear understanding of the need to articulate countersymbols that contest the rituals of oppression that dominate the lives of their constituencies. The architects of the present status quo of white supremacy and racial capitalism understand this point well, as evidenced by their continued condemnation of and repression of non-European nationalist thought (particularly black nationalism) in all its varied forms and their complete silence, or in many instances support, regarding Eurocentrism.

Unfortunately, this type of conceptual understanding has not been fully grasped by enough progressive scholars. As Michael Dawson, author of *Black Visions*, notes:

> Both a lack of appreciation for the autonomy of the black counterpublic and the ideological blinders of many scholars, which lead them to miss the significance of major nationalist movements (such as that of Marcus Garvey, of organizations such as the Nation of Islam, and of intellectuals such as Martin Delaney), contribute to the lack of theorizing about the relationship between black nationalist thought in the black counterpublic and American liberalism.[28]

In his significant work, based on what he claims to be the only major study of its kind, Dawson attempts to synthesize the disparate perspectives, but in actuality his assessment ("a lack of appreciation and ideological blinders") is an underestimation of the problem. If one examines the historical responses to black nationalism by so-called progressive scholars (at earlier periods in history, this group could be characterized as activists) it has been one of fierce antagonism. The lengths taken to stop any such movement have been endless.

The conflicting tensions around race and ideology that Douglass experiences during his lifetime prefigure historical and contemporary concerns shaping the present landscape of race and place discourse.

In 1886, Douglass wrote to his son,

> I had long been interested in ethnology, especially of the North African races. I have wanted the evidence of greatness, under a colored skin to meet and beat back the charge of natural, original and permanent

inferiority of the colored races of men. Could I have
seen forty years ago what I have now seen, I should
have been much better fortified to meet the Notts
and Gliddens... in their arguments against the negro
as a part of the great African race. Knowledge on this
subject comes to me late, but I hope not too late to be
of service; for the battle at this point is not yet fought
out, and the victory is not yet won.[29]

During the period in which Douglass visited Egypt, racial inferiority lay at the basis of evolutionary attitudes toward race.[30]
Of course, such so-called scientific racism such as that put forth
by Josiah Clark Nott[31] and George Robins Gliddon in their
infamously influential *General Remarks on Types of Mankind*
has been perpetuated by contemporary racists such as the late
Richard J. Herrnstein and Charles Murray, coauthors of the
nefarious book entitled *The Bell Curve: Intelligence and Class
Structure in American Life*, and through the type of Euroenviron-
mentalism put forth by individuals like Jared Diamond, whose
book, *Guns, Germs, and Steel: The Fates of Human Societies*, won
a Pulitzer Prize in 1997. Alfred Crosby, too, in his *The Measure
of Reality: Quantification and Western Society, 1250-1600* makes
highly imaginative claims, managing to explain the successes of
European imperialism with no mention of slavery.[32] However,
during Douglass's time, such "scientific" ideas were in their raw,
embryonic stage, yet they dominated the entire ideological spectrum as they do today.

But when Douglass witnessed the great pyramid structures,
learned of the history of great kings and queens whom he resembled, he realized then what individuals like Martin R. Delaney
and Edward Wilmot Blyden had been arguing: Africans had not
only a great history to be proud of, but this history had been systematically erased from their collective consciousness. And that
part of the process of rebuilding a national consciousness was
readjusting the lenses through which we viewed our history and

ourselves to be more properly centered around our historical and existential reality.

This is why the present discourse on race and slavery needs to be seen in its proper historical perspective. Considering that slavery was abolished in 1865, 141 years ago, the discourse on it has been slow if not dormant in its evolution. For example, no official state-sanctioned commemoration of abolition has been established; only a few postal stamps have ever been issued, nothing substantially representative of how important this historical struggle has been to what I'll refer to as *real narrative*[33] A romantic master narrative of social and racial progress has been fashioned obscuring the legacy of slavery, ever so present in our national consciousness. Even worse, so-called postmodern discourse on slavery has been constructed in such ways that the horrible institution of slavery is widely assumed to have existed without enslaved Africans and abolition having been achieved without abolitionists. Such a romantic narrative of human (racial) progress has allowed national mythologies to be constructed in ways that maintain anglocentric hegemony. A more tragic narrative is needed to explain the course of racial capitalism's development over the past five centuries.

The hidden history of resistance and abolition; the lingering legacy of antiblack racism that rose to its apex in conjunction with the development of New World slavery; the oppression that continued into the era of Jim Crow in the South after the fall of the system of chattel slavery; urban removal and gentrification that currently persist in cities across America; and the effects of global racism on people of color worldwide, particularly after World War II, when the U.S. gained military superiority within the world economic system—these are all suggestive representations of the oppression African Americans have endured.

The mass majority of Africans in America, although freed from chattel slavery, remain a loose thread in the economic, social and legal fabric of American society—barely holding on in an empire itself on the verge of collapse. The specific conditions

their ancestors struggled against have changed, yet the relationship of power between them and the dominant society, and the
ruling class that maintains the relations, remains firmly intact. If
the economic crisis is troubling, the social crisis spells doom.

The vast vestiges of slavery and institutionalized racism
coupled with the increasing ascendancy of whiteness within
America's increasingly global superstructure remain the determining factors why African Americans find themselves continuously
subjugated to the bottom of the economic order. Increasingly this
factor has received little attention among the American Left.

According to a study done by Chuck Collins and Felice
Veskel, the effects of globalization, recent changes in income and
wealth distribution, and various economic policies widened the
economic divide between a select few and the majority of Americans. They point out that "In the thirty years following World
War II, race was a principal barrier to the economic advancement for people of color."[34] But recognition of the "facts of race"
is rarely noticeable within current intellectual fashions. Instead,
African American oppression has been framed as a question of
political economy, while the racial question, the psychological
effects of racial capitalism, and the state-sponsored denigration of
the history of ex-slaves—not just on blacks, but all citizens—are
seen as marginal to the class issues that impact the larger body of
poor people in America and the world. In an attempt to avoid
engaging in what some label identity politics, many scholars have
taken this myopic approach in their discussions of race, that is,
privileging class above race as an explanation for black oppression. The inferences to be drawn from such discourse can be endlessly tragic.

WILLIAM JULIUS WILSON

In one of the most influential books on race relations of the
past two decades, *The Declining Significance of Race*,[35] its author
William Julius Wilson essentially argued that race had become
a less significant factor in the life chances and upward mobility

of African Americans. Wilson observed how jobs and capital were following whites to the suburbs, leaving behind in the cities an isolated black underclass. Because of civil rights gains, the chances of one's upward mobility had more to do with class than race, he argued.

As would be expected, his writings generated much reaction from various scholars throughout the country. The conservatives selectively borrowed from his thesis to advance their ideas about race and place, while others, including even the Association of Black Sociologists, provided harsh criticism. The latter argued that he provided "ammo" to the right-wing policy-makers whom they felt routinely propped up *individuals* to speak for *the many*. But overall, Wilson's view struck a chord, as neoliberals locked ideological arms with neoconservatives in applauding it. Two decades later, Collins and Veskel, for example, continue to echo Wilson, suggesting that "Race, while still a major factor, was diminishing as a factor in determining economic security, while class was becoming more significant."[36]

Declining Significance, complete with extensive statistics and data, strongly suggested that the problems of the African American underclass were not fundamentally due to highly racialized structural and systematic constraints, per se, but rather attitudes and irresponsibility on the part of poor blacks themselves. Such a view was all neoconservative and neoliberal whites needed to hear. Not much about *Declining Significance* was new; laissez-faire ideas amid a general welfare state critique had persisted throughout the twentieth century.[37] Wilson, however, added a fresh new twist to the debate, for few respectable commentators would argue the insignificance, or rather the declining significance, of racism in determining the life chances of African Americans as he did. Wilson, in a sense, lifted the "Negro problem" from the margins to the center of national discourse, framing the problems of the "problem people" in ahistorical terms. He attempted to deracialize the context in which black oppression and poverty took shape, in this way making it much easier for the mainstream of society to talk about. This is a difficult, if not impossible, thing to do when discussing race, but Wilson was given center stage to articulate his views.

Given the logic of Wilson's argument, the African American poor were ultimately to blame for their conditions. In an interview with Peter Werbe, Wilson was asked to elaborate on the concept, "Culture of Poverty." Dismissing such a term, he chose instead to discuss what he called "ghetto related cultural patterns."

> Soft skills, for example, are very, very important when you're interacting with middle-class black and white consumers. The extent to which you have certain personality attributes, how you relate to people in congenial ways.
>
> In inner-city neighborhoods people don't realize that often times parents will teach their children not to make eye-to-eye contact with people, particularly strangers, because you can get into trouble that way. People who make eye-to-eye contact often offend others who feel like they're "dissing" them. Or you develop a very, very tough demeanor in your interaction with people for self-protection.
>
> Those things may allow you to survive in the ghetto, but they are quite dysfunctional when you're interacting in middle-class society, because you turn people off. And, employers recognize these things.
>
> And, of course, there are real problems with the way in which kids are educated in the school systems. They graduate without the ability to read and write and speak properly, skills that are very important, particularly in the social-service sector of the economy.[38]

It isn't necessary to argue that young black males, or black females for that matter, generally do not need intensive training in the areas addressed in Wilson's comments. Problematical, however, is the way Wilson singles them out. In reality, so-called soft skills are lacking among youth of all ethnicities. Two of the most unavoidable realities experienced by African Americans collectively since the abolition of chattel slavery have been the racial discrimination experienced in attempting to find work and the racism experienced by black employees, as well as that experienced by blacks as consumers.

Many of the jobs that require the type of soft skills Wilson speaks of also discriminate against black males in their hiring practices, not because they lack soft skills, but because of their skin color. Put another way, what if the acquisition of soft skills also meant being able to communicate effectively with, say, an African American customer, or better able to relate to black employees? In other words, if we were to pretend we lived in a society that measured progress in terms of how Americans related to others across racial, gender, and class boundaries, needless to say, Anglo American whites would fare just as badly as blacks, Asians, and Latinos. But in Wilson's view, blacks are to accommodate white middle-class sensibilities; they are to acquiesce to so-called white cultural ideals and expectations that often aren't adhered to by white youth themselves. It seems to me the reason for the crisis in black male unemployment is racism. This has been the problem since the end of chattel slavery, as blacks, following behind an integrationist-minded leadership, have sought to mentally, socially, and culturally assimilate into American society.

Regarding consumer discrimination, what can be said about businesses spread out across America in all-white towns, still operating as if "whites only" signs were posted at their entrances? There are rare instances when race does not shape the interaction between black consumers and white, immigrant, and other nonblack sales persons—not to mention those operating hidden cameras. Blacks face acts of discrimination such as racialized surveillance, being overcharged, and having to often contend with open hostility from salespersons. On the other hand, as employees, black males are often subjected to hostility from customers simply for being black, and are invariably reprimanded by managers, whereas when black customers complain about customer service from whites, they are nearly always dismissed as overly sensitive and sometimes told to shop elsewhere.

Conventional wisdom attributes the crisis in black male unemployment to several factors, most notably the growing involvement of black youth in crime. Yet, as far as this issue is concerned, a recent study concluded that a white male with a felony stands a better chance of being hired than a black male with no previous criminal record. Consider the following scenario pointed out in a *Wall Street Journal* article.

> Two young high-school graduates with similar job histories and *demeanors* apply in person for jobs as waiters, warehousemen or other low-skilled positions advertised in a Milwaukee newspaper. One man is white and admits to having served 18 months in prison for possession of cocaine with intent to sell. The other is black and hasn't any criminal record.
>
> Which man is more likely to get called back? It is surprisingly close. In a carefully crafted experiment in which college students posing as job applicants visited 350 employers, the white ex-con was called back 17% of the time and the crime-free black applicant 14%. The disadvantage carried by a young black man applying for a job as a dishwasher or a driver is equivalent to forcing a white man to carry an 18-month prison record on his back.[39]

The article presents us with an interesting paradox Harry J. Holzer and Paul Offner take note of. In their essay, "The Puzzle of Black Male Unemployment," they cite the study conducted by Devah Pager of Northwestern University on black and white job applicants in Milwaukee and point out

> prison-rights advocates try to suppress the flow of information about criminal backgrounds to employers, but such a policy may actually serve to reduce young black men's chances of being hired. This

is because employers who do not check criminal
backgrounds tend to avoid hiring young black men
altogether. By contrast, when criminal background
information is available, employers can more easily
identify those who do not have criminal records, and
overall hiring of blacks increases.[40]

Indeed, if there is a common assumption that black males are
"criminal," then although their insinuation that prison advocacy
rights groups might ease up seems terribly reactionary, it does seem
to correspond more closely to the reality of black males seeking
employment; that is, if one believes that nonblacks *unknowingly*
practice discrimination when making hiring decisions.

Should we really be puzzled by the startlingly high rates of
black male unemployment? For Wilson, the government and
business elite are partly to blame, but not because of racism per
se. For him it is because of complacency and unintended neglect.
In other words, for Wilson the inability of African Americans
to achieve economic parity with whites in a post-civil rights
job market had little to do with state-sanctioned social practices, political economy, and culture within a global system of
white supremacy. Essentially, the problem of African American
unemployment rests primarily on the shoulders of black males
themselves. The underlying assumption underwriting Wilson's
argument is that American society has undergone, or has the
potential to undergo, significant progress in race relations
without significant structural adjustments. Thus, while Wilson
awaits the formation of a progressive, multiracial coalition to
take on such crises—not even a Left multiracial coalition, but
one forged within the Democratic Party—neoconservatives like
Holzer and Offner cry out for help on the behalf of black men,
whom they conclude have not fared as well in the new global
economy as their wives and sisters.

For Wilson, the main reason for blacks, particularly black
males, continuing to exhibit ghetto-related cultural patterns has
to do with suburbanization, as well as white and black middle-

class flight. Hence, he clings to a Darwinian-inspired and assimilationist idea that essentially argues that if whites would resettle the inner cities—and we could assume the black middle class would follow them—things would be better for the blacks, for they would now have role models, social values, jobs, and housing available to them.

Cynthia Hamilton's essay, "From Streets of Hope to Landscapes of Despair: The Case of Los Angeles," provides a more realistic picture of what has transpired within the majority of urban landscapes in America. She argues that land-use planning and zoning have been the most decisive factors in determining public space and, thus, political and social behavior:

> Decisions about the use of land have retarded social justice and created racial, ethnic, and class conflict in American cities. These decisions have resulted in the deterioration of Black communities through displacement and redevelopment. Historically, Black communities have offered alternative sources of identity and meaning for life in America. These places, as suggested by some observers, were sources of support and assistance for residents and maintained control and order based on shared values. Order disappeared along with community and the artificial replacement (through the use of police, courts, and prisons) is far too costly for the well-being of communities.[41]

One only needs to tour any neighborhood in the United States where African Americans are concentrated to experience Hamilton's astute observation. In the course of three decades, these "places" have been racially gentrified. People who once inhabited these "alternative" places have had their own welcoming mats removed from under them, and are subjected to policing, housing discrimination, and racial reaction. The manner in which gentrification has unfolded in cities across America resembles the destruction of rain forests, where various villages, not to mention important animal species, can become endangered overnight.

The rationale for such inhumane treatment could only be found in the logic of white supremacy, the simple belief that the people residing in these communities are not worthy of human compassion. The main problem with gentrification isn't that Anglo Americans migrate into black communities to share space, but that most often they collectively perpetuate the same frontier mentality that existed during the so-called ages of discovery and westward expansion, or Hitler's *lebensraum*. The inner cities of America have been recaptured, jobs have moved back, and the significance of race has "declined" by virtue of the dwindling black presence resulting from the escalating wave of "urban renewal." Increasingly, urban renewal seems to signal a prelude to genocide.

BILL CLINTON, WILLIAM JULIUS WILSON, AND VERNON JORDAN

I am not suggesting Wilson's work had any significant bearing on the outlook of various antiracist activists, or that it achieved any ideological saliency within the grassroots where they worked. In fact, most serious-minded activists were undeterred by the illusions of racial progress. The absence of a strongly organized progressive movement, however, allows for the ideas put forth by academics like Wilson—no matter how farfetched—to achieve much greater resonance. For Democratic elite party operatives, Wilson's perspective made a lot of sense and fits well within the Democratic Leadership Conference's[42] scheme to implement, as Robert C. Smith terms it, "non-race-specific public policies."[43] Former president Bill Clinton had nothing but praise for Wilson's *Declining Significance*, saying that it gave him a much clearer understanding of race and poverty and the problems of the inner city. Of Wilson's *The Truly Disadvantaged*, Clinton wrote that by 1988, "I had become a convert to William Julius Wilson's argument, that there were no race-specific solutions to hard-core unemployment and poverty. The only answers were schools, adult education and training, and jobs."[44]

Political scientists Ronald Walters and Robert C. Smith note in their book *African American Leadership,* "By the time that President Clinton ran successfully for the presidency in 1992,[Wilson's] view of black poverty was the dominant one in Washington political and policy circles.... Clinton campaigned on the theme of 'personal responsibility'... and a promise to 'end welfare as we know it,'"[45] marking the end of a long, drawn-out divorce proceeding between the Democratic Party establishment and its leftover coalition of New Deal activists and "Jesse Jackson" Democrats. Clinton wasn't directing his message to corporations like Enron and Arthur Andersen, but was simply embellishing America's preexisting historical script, which always blames its victims, particularly if those victims happened to be American blacks or immigrants of African descent.

Who could forget the surreal State of the Union speech Clinton delivered to the nation four years after the welfare reform act of 1996 was enacted under his leadership? Appearing to break away from his script, Clinton hinted to the practically all-white assembly of elected officials, "I believe one of the reasons the American people gave me a second term was to take the tough decisions in the next four years that will carry our country through the next fifty years." He went on to touch on the issue of campaign finance reform, urging his colleagues to pass the bipartisan McCain-Feingold bill by July 4, or as he put it, "the day we celebrate the birth of our democracy." But how many Americans think fifty years ahead while deciding whom to vote for? How many Americans knew the ruling class had a fifty-year plan?

Clinton was responding to the ruling class's sensibilities to the "Negro problem." The system of welfare was seen as one of the last pillars of "big government" and "social spending." With the move toward privatization of the economy and the prison industrial complex presented as an alternative, welfare was viewed as an impediment to progress. However, although the welfare and campaign finance reform have been viewed as divisive issues, the specter of the United States becoming a prison state has gone unnoticed in congressional debates.

Throughout his presidency, Bill Clinton regularly stage-managed his association with high-profile African American intellectuals like Harvard professor Henry Louis Gates and Wilson. The most prominent figure of course was Vernon E. Jordan, a well-known civil rights leader who played an important role during the 1970s of "integrating" the boards of major corporations and lobbying for affirmative action in the private sector. Having known and advised Clinton for more than a decade, Jordan headed his presidential transition team during the inaugural period of his presidency and later stayed on as a member of the "Kitchen Cabinet."

Jordan's antipathy toward black radicalism is revealed in his autobiography, as he recalls in an anecdote an encounter he had with a young black militant in the elevator:

> The Urban League did have generally favorable experiences with the Nixon administration, although my *open* association with Ehrlichman raised eyebrows in some quarters. *The press took note of our tennis dates.* One day, on my way to work, a young black man with a big Afro, dressed in a dashiki, confronted me in the elevator at the League office.
> "Good morning," I said.
> "Mr. Jordan, I'm glad to see you because I want to say something to you."
> "Yes?"
> "You can't be my leader playing tennis at the White House with John Ehrlichman."
> "Which federal program are you on?" I asked.
> "The Labor Education Advancement Program."
> "How much do you make?"
> "Twenty thousand a year."
> I said, "I'm playing tennis with John Ehrlichman so you can continue to be a $20,000-a-year militant. Do you understand that?"

Jordan leaves the reader with the impression that militants were simply ghetto hustlers leeching off the backs of the more main-stream black leadership.[46] When, in fact, the opposite was closer to the truth. Programs such as the Labor Education and other War on Poverty programs were the direct result of the militant struggles of working-class people; this includes the perverted ideology of black power put forth by Nixon's administration and the black bourgeoisie leadership class.[47] That is, Lyndon B. Johnson's War on Poverty, Nixon's championing of black capital-ism, and the government's initiation of such programs as Labor Education were designed to circumvent the rising tide of black resistance during the late 1960s and early 1970s.

I would much rather have had Jordan turn the script around, instead having the militant in the elevator saying to him, "I'm wearing this dashiki and big Afro so that you can have your job as head Negro in charge of controlling the political direction of black militancy." While it might seem as if I'm nit-picking at Jordan, my point is that it is terribly disingenuous on the part of many black leaders to ridicule any aspect of the tradition of black struggle for liberation and freedom—most certainly not the militant nationalist tradition. Not all militants were employed within Labor Education and War on Poverty, many were impris-oned, exiled, neutralized; others simply capitulated in order to survive. Some have become outstanding educators in many of the finest educational institutions in America.

As a matter of historical record, it should be known that while Jordan was riding up and down corporate elevators and playing tennis with Ehrlichman, the U.S. government was waging a relentless military war against militant leadership and various black communities. My point here, though, is to simply put Jor-dan's reactionary outlook in a context. In his essay, "Black Power in the International Context," the late Larry Neal made the fol-lowing observation; it is worth quoting at length:

The present-day Negro leadership has no independent international position because it does not see
the struggle in nationalist terms. And that is why it
is dangerous. It is important not to fall into the trap
of simply labeling these leaders as Uncle Toms. It is
imperative that we have a clear understanding of the
manner in which they view the world. This is the only
way to fight them. They speak for thousands of Black
people, and the failure of the militants to understand
the reasons for that appeal would be disastrous. Psy-
chologically, black America is conflicted about seeing
itself as an integral part of American society. DuBois
referred to this phenomenon as "double consciousness." This double consciousness has been implicit
in the black man's history since the first slaves were
brought here four hundred years ago. The struggle
within the race has centered around the correct
manner in which to destroy this double consciousness. Or in more precise political terms, it has been
an internal struggle between the nationalist and the
integrationists.

The integrationists do not believe that the basic
socio-economic structure must be destroyed. But
rather, that Negroes must simply be given a greater
slice of the capitalistic action. They believe in reform
not revolution. They are men who are essentially
awed by the power of the Establishment. They have
weighed the issues and decided that the best course
lies in seeking some kind of rapprochement with the
"system." The system is not bad at heart, they say, it
just does not have enough black people in key jobs
and fine houses.[48]

Jordan's political outlook and behavior exemplify this tradition of assimilationist ideology, which has been allowed to develop
unimpeded by the dictates of counterintelligence programs. As
Neal later noted, their presence and visibility have global implica-

tions. One should never expect a leader such as Jordan to interject in any form or fashion with American foreign policy, even when such policies are morally wrong. Jordan's background, his political trajectory, places him at odds with the tradition of black radicalism, and he makes certain this is clear for his readers.

Rather than accept an actual cabinet position, Jordan chose instead to become a figurehead for a variety of reasons, most notably financial, as he would have been forced to forego some of his lucrative entrepreneurial goals. Interestingly, Bill Clinton notes in his autobiography that he had hoped to appoint Vernon Jordon to the attorney general post, but Jordan refused. What was the meaning of his symbolic representation (to borrow a useful term from Columbia Professor Manning Marable) within White House inner circles? It should have been clear to most that Jordan's role was to lend legitimacy to Clinton's agenda, and oftentimes this required going along with policies that obviously ran counter to the interests of African Americans. As Jordan's autobiography reveals, this presented no dilemma for him. After all, the press took note of his playing golf with the president.

The major themes defining Clinton's two terms as U.S. president were not the Monica Lewinsky scandal, the war in Kosovo where he assembled an international military coalition to defeat Slobodan Milosevic's government in Yugoslavia, or his self-proclaimed brilliant economic plan. Clinton's greatest accomplishments for the ruling class were his successes in pushing through both the crime bill and welfare reform legislation. Each directly impacted African American communities in tragic tandem, serving as a template for the subsequent attempts by the Bush administration to reform Social Security. Yet there was very little opposition on the part of black leadership to the implementation of these draconian policies. Carefully allying himself with various establishment blacks throughout his two terms in office, Clinton rarely had to deal with any substantial criticism from highly visible African American public intellectuals, and the public was always under the impression that certain African American leaders had his ear. A great many even believed that Clinton himself was an African American passing for "white."

So crafty were Clinton's media spinmasters in casting him as a "new" southerner who understood the plight of African Americans, that it would be impossible to argue that many of the decisions he made actually put him in good company with the far-right wing or at least blurred the lines of distinction. As for Jordan, the news media took particular notice of him driving Clinton around on a golf course.

Gates, Wilson, and Jordan—and there were others—became fully integrated into what political scientist Michael Dawson has referred to as the "new regime of race-relations management," except neither of these three were elected by the constituencies they supposedly represent; they are more or less hypermanagers, with no real significant power to influence anything but image. Although it was widely believed Clinton had earlier sought out Wilson's advice in formulating economic policies, when Wilson voiced opposition to his signing of the draconian Welfare Reform Act in 1996, it was clear to those following the trajectory of his career that his own *significance* had declined in White House circles.

Wilson seemed to think progress had been made, as exemplified by a growing black middle class, yet his thesis didn't occur in an intellectual vacuum. It is interesting to note that in 1978, the year *Declining Significance* was originally published, Robert B. Hill, then director of research for the National Urban League, issued this report: *The Illusion of Black Progress*.[49] Similar to Hill's study, *Declining Significance* included significant data, yet Wilson's focus led him toward conclusions that strongly contradicted Hill's. For example, Hill noted that "Between 1975 and 1976, the black to white family income ratio fell sharply from 62 to 59 percent" (p. iv). His findings included the following: Black unemployment was at its highest level and the jobless gap between whites and blacks at its widest; the jobless rate had grown from 1.7 times that of whites at the peak of the 1975 recession to 2.3 times by the first half of 1978; the proportion of middle-income black families had not increased significantly; the proportion of black families living above the government's higher budget had dropped from 12 to 9 percent; that the proportion of black families with incomes under $7,000, as well as those with incomes over $15,000, remained relatively constant; and that statistical evidence strongly contradicted the assumption that persistent high unemployment among black youth was primarily due to their educational or skill deficiencies, and that job opportunities had been made available to white youth with lower educational attainment.[50]

Scholarship is a very subjective endeavor; individuals can share the same data yet draw completely different interpretations. Such was the case with social scientists during the decade immediately following the civil rights movement. Some greatly exaggerated the gains of the Movement, and for this they were given high visibility within the establishment's intellectual and media apparatus; while others able to see through the smoke and mirrors were completely marginalized, discredited, and rarely heard from or seen in public.[51] Perhaps Wilson, now a world-renowned economic professor, was one of those captivated by this grand illusion of progress. Besides co-opting academics with various research rewards and prestige, another key strategy of the ruling class's enlisting consent among African Americans was to rely on 'Hollywood' in constructing the imagery of black representation. One shouldn't assume that black academicians were immune to such sophistry.

Coinciding with this new direction in black representation was the fact that by 1980, the number of African American elected officials had increased considerably. African Americans were much more visible in the arts and entertainment world, which itself had been rapidly transformed by the developments in information technology. Blacks were made much more visible, and for many there was a growing sense that progress was being made, as reflected in Henry Louis Gates's comments:

> ours was the first generation to attend integrated
> schools in the wake of *Brown v. Board*; to have
> watched, as children, the dismantling of Jim Crow
> and to wonder where the process might end; to
> be given the chance, through affirmative action,
> to compete against white boys and girls; to enter
> and integrate the elite institutions just as the most
> expansive notions of radical democracy made an
> entrance.[52]

To be sure, although there existed a widening gap between the
African American and white middle class, there was economic
growth among an increasing number of blacks nonetheless; there
was enough increased mobility to provide the illusion that progress was being made, particularly if one was measuring progress in
individual terms and not in relation to the broader community's
collective interests.[53] Gates, however, fails to fully if at all engage
the response of the non-African American public to these perceived changes in representation, as they were also affected by
the reconfigured dynamics of race and class. And by non-African
Americans, I am not simply referring to Anglo Americans.

America's cultural reach, due to television and film, was
pervasive in an unprecedented fashion, and for the first time in
history the stereotypical images of blacks penetrated the living
rooms of millions of people in the United States as well as hundreds of countries abroad. This new form of black, or African
American, representation invariably evaded the racism blacks
encountered daily and, as such, helped to foster the romantic
narrative of progress. Television shows began to focus less on
the cultural divide between white and black America, instead
emphasizing the class divide within the black community.

All in a single night one could watch on television the *Cosby
Show*, which portrayed the life and times of a black bourgeois
family, and any nightly news, which regularly included segments
devoted exclusively to reporting on black criminal activity. Or
they could indulge themselves in the postmodern minstrelsy that

characterized so much of the popular rap acts. One would logically conclude from TV programs like the *Cosby Show*, for example, that blacks had made great strides, while also concluding after a few encounters with the nightly news that young black males were basically criminal, prone to ghetto-related cultural patterns. How is it that you have individuals like "Dr. Huxtable," the patriarch of the fictionalized *Cosby Show* family, if not for the progress we've made in race-relations? Why would an individual like "Skip" (Henry Louis Gates's nickname) complain about racism if he's reaped the benefits of American liberalism? Perhaps there is something wrong with the majority of them, for if "Dr. Huxtable" and "Skip" can make it because of their humor and genius, then it must be due to other shortcomings—perhaps cultural—that the others lag so ineradicably far behind. The fact is that despite the increasing electoral victories and the increase in life chances of achieving middle-class lifestyles, for the majority of African Americans life in the United States was one big plantation.

THE COLOR LINE IS THE POWER LINE IS THE POVERTY LINE

Turning our attention back to Wilson, I believe there are factors he completely missed, this largely due to the limited ideological lenses he used in focusing his study. Wilson represents a school of thought highly distrustful of the legacies of both black power and its broader implications: the 1968 revolution, which forced empire to change face. For him the rise of conservatism resulted from black power militants sabotaging the civil rights movement, polarizing African and Anglo Americans. In a subtle manner, he advocated a volte-face on the part of the movement, which he felt had been overrun by black militants whose influence in the large urban areas was less important because the "political power and influence of the cities are on the wane."[54]

Given the present gentrification of urban inner cities throughout the country and the mass removal and consequent displacement and containment of poor African Americans—especially since the passage of various welfare reform laws—Wilson's argument seems incredibly flawed. Of course, this is all in hindsight.[55] In all fairness, the term "big government" had not yet been demonized by the fascists who now control the government and media when his study was done; liberalism, multiracial democracy, and social welfare programs had not yet been discredited by the logic of their own contradictions.

Few post-New Deal presidents, if any, proved as committed to social reform as Jimmy Carter. In hindsight we now realize that Carter was a staunch conservative with regard to foreign policy, but at the time (when one could still smell the stench of "Whites Only" signs), his social liberalism on most domestic issues, most notably affirmative Action, helped sustain the faith many African American leaders had increasingly placed in government.[56] Additionally, although today the Democratic Party appears as one arm of the emperor's unclothed body (the GOP being the other), one would be hard-pressed to notice any semblance between the two during a period in history when the Barry Goldwaters of the world shaped the GOP policies and its strategists—for example, implementing the subsequent 1968 "southern strategy," which saw the party's full-scale retreat from civil rights issues to one altogether committed to accommodating the sons, daughters, and grandchildren of the Confederacy. Strangely, it is within the context of these two prevailing factors that mainstream African American leadership between the late 1960s and early 1970s decided the Democratic Party represented the most, if not the only, effective channel for advancing the interests of their constituencies.

While Wilson's thesis was being debated among academic intellectuals within the nation's ivory towers, and among Democratic Party aficionados, there was a rise in neoconservatism within the general public, as reflected in the election of Ronald Reagan. The consequences of Reagan's tenure have been termed by progressives as "Reaganomics." In general, Reaganomics meant tax breaks, loosening of environmental regulations, corporate welfare for the rich, as well as cutbacks in social spending, public education, and jobs programs for the poor—setting the stage for vicious attacks on civil rights and more specifically affirmative action and welfare reform.

George Winslow, in his book *Capital Crimes*, illustrates how the elite played their part in the Reagan revolution by cultivating popular opinion to support their economic and political interests, contributing billions of dollars to political officials, subsidizing the religious fundamentalists, and supporting an elaborate, multilayered campaign against immigrants of color, blacks, and poor alike.[57] The world in which we live—that is, one shaped by the dictates of a "War on Terrorism"—is the logical culmination of events set in motion during this pivotal period in American history.

As Winslow's study concludes, Reagan's revolution, however grand the scheme appears to have been, failed short in its goals. It did not end with Reagan's departure from the White House. At the conclusion of Reagan's presidency, African American poverty was well past the 50 percent mark, and as George H. W. Bush entered the White House numerous African American communities were completely devastated by poverty, the drug epidemic,[58] and a complete absence of effective leadership. Still, the conditions would eventually deteriorate even further; the coldest winter of all was yet to come.

Contrary to popular opinion, Clinton's presidency did little to counteract the rising tide of conservatism. In fact, his presidency simply masked over the systemic structures of racial inequality indelibly tied into the historical development of neoliberal hegemony. Clinton's presidency expropriated much of the Christian fundamentalist and elite's agendas for law and order, corporate welfare, and the globalization of racial capitalism. It should not have been surprising to anyone that between 1980 and 2000, the number of people in prisons, jails, on parole, and on probation increased threefold, nor should the fact that African Americans made up half the prison inmate population. Today, more than one-third of young black men are either locked away behind fences, on parole, or on probation, but little pressure was brought to bear upon the Clinton administration during his term in office. Even worse to consider is the fact that more than 70 percent of the individuals sentenced to prisons in 1998 were nonviolent offenders, and the rate of African American women's imprisonment is increasing at a rate three times that of their male counterparts. If all goes as planned, the adverse effects of Clinton's "law and order" policies will be felt for perhaps fifty years or more, and given the present trends of incarceration, 2053 will mark another turning point: the majority of American citizens will be locked behind bars.

The draconian policies implemented during the so-called Reagan-Bush era not only continued uninterrupted during the first Bush's presidency, but the severity was intensified during Clinton's. As head of the conservative policy group, Democratic Leadership Conference, Clinton helped to craft an agenda that would resonate across party lines, leading to the support for the construction of more prisons, ending welfare, increasing policing and surveillance, and new forms of suppressing dissent. The devastating consequences of liberal capitalism and the unwillingness of the black petit bourgeois leadership class to put forth an alternative vision of politics provides an enduring lesson for black radical leadership. No longer can a radical agenda be entwined within the rubric of Democratic Party ideology; no longer can the argument that the election of a Democratic president will at least forestall the excesses of the far-right wing be taken seriously.

The fact is that absent real and concrete challenges to the myriad contradictions inherent in an essentially two-party system, social and political expectations have been forced to exist at low ebb. This has been especially true in the present period, where since the pivotal year 1968 there have been few visibly serious contestations against empire from the political left. There were some moments in 1989, such as the fall of apartheid in South Africa and the little known student rebellions throughout the country, of which the late cultural worker Toni Cade Bambara numbered at over 200 in a speech delivered in Dallas, Texas in 1990.[59] But such rebellions proved to be illusory at best, as they occurred outside the context of a social and political movement.

Nikhil Pal Singh, a Washington University professor of history, in his essay titled "Toward an Effective Antiracism," must have had the Wilsons, Al Gores, Bill Clintons, Bob Borosages, Ann Lewiss and Jesse Jacksons of the world in mind when he suggested that

> Others, more disingenuous, have argued that in order to again gain influence, American liberals and leftists must put aside racial questions altogether, since by aligning progressive ideas under the banner of anti-racism liberalism has done little more than alienate itself from a 'silent majority' of Americans and initiate a "blacklash" that has pushed this country on a more or less continuous rightward course since the late 1960s.[60]

Singh correctly points out that these attempts are insufficient to withstand the combination of neoliberal social policy assaults and "neoracist common sense" that have held their footing over the past two decades. Past two decades?

Antiracist movements must conceive of racism as a permanent feature of racial empire, and any attempts to avoid confronting this enduring fact will only invite present and future pitfalls. Africans, from the time of their forced entry into the New World as a commodity, have been denied citizenship, autonomy, self-determination, and the self-activity necessary for social development while at the same time suffering an enduring social and representational crisis. Liberalism and certainly conservatism have never been able to address the full range of problems confronting African people in the United States. It should be a foregone conclusion that the status quo establishment will concede nothing without radical demands put forth by an organized and mobilized group of people.

Political, racial, and social subjugation, and economic subjugation as well, have been the most defining features characterizing African presence within the United States. It can probably be argued successfully that racism has been the central accompaniment to capitalism's development in the New World, as well as its expansion abroad. More than 500 years since Columbus's landfall in the Americas, skin color remains the fundamental human characteristic delineating those who are exploiters and exploited. A. Sivanandan is correct:

> Today, under capitalism—capitalism without contradictions, capitalism without communities to stand up against it, without race and class movements, without Third World revolutions—the color line is the power line is the poverty line. Those who are poor—and are powerless to do anything about their poverty—are also those who, by and large, are non white, non western, Third World.[61]

LOUIS FARRAKHAN, MANNING MARABLE, AND CORNEL WEST

Among prominent Left public intellectuals there seems to be little agreement on the extent of African American oppression—or the reason for it. If one has followed public debates over a period of time, they might accurately conclude that, for many of these public intellectuals who identify themselves as Leftists, their position on any given issue depends largely on which side of the bed they awaken. Many of the most prominent public intellectuals vacillate on various issues because their primary concern is not social change as much as personal, and increasingly class, legitimization, and representation. Few visible commentators, most of whom are located within (or connected with through philanthropic patronage) the very institutions of power that maintain and perpetuate racial capitalist hegemony, have been able to articulate the ubiquitous nature of contemporary African American oppression in a manner that resonates clearly because to challenge the orthodoxy, to veer beyond the ideological boundaries they have been trained to navigate, is to risk losing one's credibility not with the masses but with the American Left establishment, whose approval their careers often depend upon or to whom they feel a sense of allegiance for helping them place their foot inside the door. Meanwhile, they seem to be literally unaffected by the fact that the collective grievances of African Americans have been met with recalcitrant resistance by not only the government and its socially conservative electoral base, but also the general population and the so-called Left.

Reform government programs like affirmative action, designed to ensure employment growth among minorities; the multicultural arguments put forth by academic intellectuals for cultural recognition; small symbolic gestures such as the inclusion of other groups whose narratives have traditionally been excluded into textbooks and educational curriculum; the protests for removal of racist symbols like the Confederate flag from property supported by a multiracial tax base; these demands—all of which if adhered to, would merely amount to tokenism—have been soundly rebuffed in popular discourse, and state intervention has been absent. Contemporary antiracist efforts void of historicity and intended to reverse the dangerous effects of racism are increasingly seen in the popular imagination as "reverse racism" emanating from a "culture of complaint." It is a sad commentary on contemporary intellectualism that discourses around such issues have sunken to such lowly depths.

By attempting to frame their arguments against economic inequality in ways that ignore the racialized context in which racism has historically functioned, neoliberals as well as Left intellectuals have interlocked with neoconservatives in constructing a discourse that essentially trivializes the impact of racism, the enslavement of Africans, and antiblack modes of state and vigilante repression. Can one seriously believe that the American Left has a program that will improve the life chances of African Americans (the majority of whom are merely denizens) and put the country on a course where the elimination of racial inequality in a capitalist-driven economy is foreseeable? Perhaps there is a reason for this continuous divide. Who should we blame?

For some time it has become intellectually fashionable for African American public intellectuals to establish their mainstream credentials by publicly attacking more popular and grassroots-oriented leadership. The most noticeable example of this has been the contemptuous criticism of Minister Louis Farrakhan, leader of the Nation of Islam (NOI), an organization headquartered in Chicago with satellite mosques in most metropolitan cities throughout the United States. Manning Marable's central critique of Farrakhan, for example, is that he rejects integration as a political strategy. Farrakhan's political program, according to Marable, is echoic of Garvey's nationalism during the first quarter of the twentieth century. "He represents a kind of Black authoritarianism that can't be tolerated and can't be accepted as any kind of program to advance Black issues and interests," says Marable in an interview published in the book *Talking About a Revolution*.[62] This is strange talk when one considers that Marable views himself in the tradition of Malcolm X, the symbolic founder of modern black nationalism.

Interestingly, Marable's criticisms of Farrakhan are reminiscent of DuBois's vicious attacks on Garvey; most of them focus on issues of marginal importance, and have mostly to do with personality. However, the following assessment of Farrakhan in his book *Beyond Black and White* reveals an even more problematical pattern in Marable's thinking:

> As white Americans moved right, the political culture of black America became fertile terrain for the reactionary agenda of conservative black nationalism and the resurgence of Louis Farrakhan. Black support for Farrakhan has less to do with his odious anti-Semitism or narrow and dogmatic sexism, than his unique ability to express the rage and frustration of broad sectors of the urban underclass. Thus

> African-Americans may reject the bigotry of the
> Nation of Islam, but nevertheless feel that Farrakhan
> expresses some important ideas reflecting the mood
> of the community.[63]

Marable here is relieving the African American community of its historical agency, suggesting that its collective ideological orientation (here, he is generalizing, not me) is primarily determined by the movements and dictates of white America. "Fertile terrain for a reactionary agenda," writes Marable, inferring that if capitalism was perhaps a bit more benevolent in its repression, blacks might be more susceptible to anything other than an ideology that compels them to work together politically, socially, and economically. "Less to do with his odious ..." infers that the alleged anti-Semitism and sexism of Farrakhan is partly the reason for his prominence within the black community.

In fact, Marable's stubborn insistence that Farrakhan is odiously anti-Semitic and sexist seems to me far too acquiescent to those Zionist elements within the Jewish community who have figured prominently in cultivating antiblack and Arab Palestinian politics.

But what is most deeply troubling is the manner in which the significance of Farrakhan's ability to articulate clarity on issues that cut across class lines within the black community, and the programs the Nation of Islam have historically implemented within urban communities across America, are routinely trivialized as mere footnotes. Any cursory analysis of the present NOI membership or individuals who critically approve of his views would reveal a representation far removed from that presented by Marable. As in other organizations (churches, NAACP, the Urban League, sports teams, etc.) there will be automatons, people who follow blindly. I know for fact there are members of the NOI who await the Mother Ship, who feel Farrakhan is beyond criticism. But I would assume most individuals join the organization because it provides for them a seemingly more progressive alternative to the traditional organizations, such as churches, civil rights organizations, and so on.

The NOI's membership is comprised of individuals very much in tune with an uplift ideology akin to that of other traditional groups like the various African American sororities and fraternities; and a great deal of its leadership seems to derive from such fraternal origins. The present NOI functions as a sort of alternative "talented tenth," or perhaps more youth-oriented "five percent," and stands ready to guide the masses to freedom. Its high visibility in the areas where black people collectively reside is another reason for its attractiveness. The community is more likely to witness a minister in the organization responding to a highly charged racial conflict, an instance of police abuse, or any other type of injustice perpetrated against the community. They're even likely to see members of the NOI at a political rally. Also, for those who are "listening" to Farrakhan, that he appears to speak independently of the establishment lends weight to his significance as a heroic figure. Unlike many of the monkeys we are accustomed to observing, one has to look much harder to discern the organ grinders behind Farrakhan's curtain.

Without the slightest hint of embarrassment, Marable writes in *Beyond Black and White* that "one prominent white publisher explained to him, 'We would rather have a black leadership which *goes nowhere*, than a black progressive leadership which talks to Farrakhan.'"[64] It seems that Marable, like the younger DuBois of the Garvey Era, would rather blacks remain under the present conditions of servitude rather than see Farrakhan play a prominent role in black politics. Farrakhan is not the black messiah but sadly enough, the Nation of Islam is one of the most organized and disciplined group of Africans in the diaspora. In addition, it is probably more decentralized (or perhaps less centralized) than any of the mainstream civil rights organizations, more accountable to its constituency than any of the white left organizations are (or even profess to be) to the African American community; I am certain that it functions more democratically than Columbia University, or, as Cornel West might agree, Harvard. As of yet, the Nation of Islam has not been called upon to police the African American community as some sort of paramilitary type of infantry.

Former Harvard University professor Cornel West takes a similar approach. In an interview with *Tikkun* editor Michael Lerner on the subject of black nationalism, West is asked by the Jewish rabbi to distinguish between a narrow black nationalist and a progressive black nationalist. West responds, "A progressive black nationalist is like a progressive Zionist.... They are, rather, the prophetic critics of their fellow nationalists."[65] I really feel the term progressive Zionist needs to be defined, but this doesn't happen, unless we take the statement at its face value. Lerner then, in a manner of astonishing audaciousness, poses the question, "How can we get people to spend less time listening to Farrakhan and more time listening to progressive people?" West answers:

> We've got to institutionalize progressive voices in both communities so that they become more visible and effective. There are a number of persons who right now sympathize with and even follow Minister Farrakhan, who in the early part of the twenty-first century will be radical democrats. These people are fundamentally concerned about black suffering; they go into Farrakhan's organization because they are concerned about this suffering and in the end they feel that it doesn't provide enough vision and insight and analysis. So they end up as progressives. This is the trajectory of persons such as Malcolm X, Amiri Baraka, Sonia Sanchez. There is a struggle going on over the minds, bodies and souls of young black Americans, some of whom will go through Minister Louis Farrakhan's organizations and end up as progressives. How soon? It's hard to say. The progressive black nationalist position is the closest I come to, although I personally don't consider myself a nationalist of any sort.[66]

West's flat-footed response would give the blues the blues, and one even wonders why he would publish it, particularly when in the afterword to *Cornel West: A Critical Reader,* he writes so favorably of black nationalism:

> My critical appreciation of the Black nationalist tra-
> dition goes back to *Prophecy Deliverance!*, where the
> African Blood Brotherhood, Black Panther Party, and
> League of Revolutionary Black Workers are heralded
> as high moments in the Black Freedom Struggle. This
> stance has been consistent in my work, as witnessed
> by my sustained engagement and debates with the
> Dean of Contemporary Black Nationalism, my dear
> brother Maulana Karenga, the leading Black national-
> ist, the beloved Minister Louis Farrakhan, the tower-
> ing scholar of Pan African Studies, the late and great
> John Henrik Clarke, and the famous theorist of Afro-
> centrism, my fellow co-teacher Molefi Asante.[67]

Sifting through the fragmented historical trajectory of West's career as a public intellectual to locate some sense of coherency would be like moving a mountain with a mustard seed. True enough West is a Renaissance scholar, an expert on nearly all things. Consistent, however, is his belief that nationalism and Marxism are but stepping stones to his fantastic sense of a progressive community of resistance. West's and Marable's views, however, are simply "in line" with the American new Left, which as a whole has never comprehended the significance of black nationalism and has always been opposed to independent black movements, and quite frankly, as a whole, uncaring of black sufferings.

An examination of the history of black nationalism in the late nineteenth and early twentieth centuries reveals an ongoing tension between independently run organizations, self-assertive individuals, and the white Left. Consider the political trajectory of these activist/intellectuals, from Marxist-Trotskyite leanings to radical egalitarian forms of pan-Africanism—Hubert Harrison, George Padmore, W.E.B. DuBois, C.L.R. James, Kwame Ture—

the list goes on, and the experiences of these individuals are quite telling. Each, in his unique way, grew frustrated with the prospects of achieving a multiracial democracy in America through the traditional methods of seeking organizational alliances with the white left. As Jeffrey B. Perry points out in *A Hubert Harrison Reader*,

> Socialist theory and practice, including segregated locals in the South, the failure to route the campaign of the 1912 presidential candidate Eugene V. Debs through the South, racist positions on Asian immigration at the 1912 national convention, and the failure to support the[Colored Socialist Club] politically and economically soon led Harrison to conclude that Socialist Party leaders, like organized labor, put the white "race first and class after."[68]

Harrison's "race first" was not narrow nationalism in the sense that liberals use the term today; it was the logical intellectual and activist response to white racism.

George Padmore, according to the venerable theorist C.L.R. James, was one of the most powerful black men of his time. Of Padmore, James said to an audience in 1971, "I don't believe any black man up to that time had held any position of such power and authority because he had the finances and the international organization of the Communist International at his disposal."[69] Indeed Padmore is a towering and eminent icon in the history of African struggles for liberation. His books *How Britain Rules Africa* and *Pan Africanism or Communism* are both classic texts, yet Padmore's significance derives not from what he wrote, but from his skills as an organizer.[70] James, in the same speech, says Padmore remained a Marxist until his death—that was his method—but he believed black organizations should be independent of white outside control. Padmore was a Marxist with an *experience*, as James put it:

> And his idea was when you join these people, they use you for their own purposes. George did not

> think in terms of race. He was one of the persons
> least touched by race prejudice. He understood these
> large European organizations—Communist Party,
> Trade Union Organizations—as not too different
> from liberals and the rest of them in that they were
> national organizations devoted to the development
> of the intellectual and political persons of white
> people....And when you joined them they saw you as
> a subordinate, inferior and contributing to what they
> were doing.[71]

Malcolm X came to the same conclusion, according to James, when he formed the Organization for African American Unity. Although for most Americans, Stokely Carmichael is viewed as the fiery leader of the Student Nonviolent Coordinating Committee (SNCC), the dominant media apparatus doesn't highlight the fact that he would eventually shed his master's name for Kwame Ture, and immigrate to the continent of Africa where he became an ambassador for the All African People's Revolutionary Party—scientific socialism was his method.

Marxism may have been for Cornel West "the brook of fire—the purgatory—of our postmodern times," but history has borne out the near inevitability of nationalism being the mountaintop in regard to intellectual awakening among activist leaders. Fortunately, there is still room at the cross for Marable. But he needs to seriously come to grips with the fact that the problem confronting the building of a movement is not Farrakhan. But let's not get too carried away with labels; none of these individuals mentioned above defined themselves solely as black nationalists, and it would be a grave mistake to simply lump their names squarely alongside that of Farrakhan. Nevertheless, Farrakhanism does represent a form of nationalism. His organization, the Nation of Islam, is a nationalist organization. It is for this reason he is attacked by liberals, the Left, and their African American representatives such as West, Marable, and others. Criticisms of Farrakhan rarely stem from the relationship he has with the black community but instead from his relationship to white society.

What then, is black nationalism? It is essentially the uniting of people of African descent based on our common culture, historical circumstances, and present condition. The unifying thread tying black people together in America is their historical and contemporary relationship to white society, as well as their shared cultural heritage, which derives primarily from West Africa. Black people live in an antiblack society. Slavery, Jim Crow, and contemporary racism were, and are, lived experiences among the vast majority of black Americans. Black nationalism is also a concerted effort to overcome black self-hatred by instilling love for self and community in its place. But in a "post-civil rights" era, such an ideological construction appears outdated. This seems to me, however, to be the one moment in history where black political leadership must come to grips with the question at hand. Where do *we* go from here? Or, where do *some of us* go from here?

Gates argues, for example, that black America is more fissured than white America (he presents no evidence to back such a grandiose claim): The "mounting intraracial disparities mean that the realities of race no longer affect all blacks in the same way. There have been perverse consequences: In part to assuage our sense of survivor's guilt, we often cloak these differences in a romantic black nationalism—something that has become the veritable socialism of the black bourgeoisie."[72] His outlook isn't as new as even he might think; he's not the first black antiblack nationalist on the block. In my opinion, Gates and many of his contemporaries are simply obsessed with the tasks of explaining themselves, bolstering their sense of self-importance, and rationalizing their deepening estrangement from the majority black community in the purgatory of their American dreams. Sadly, however, this faction of elitist black leadership holds the upper hand in black political discourse.

This coupled with the failure of the American Left—and by this I'm including its constellation of African American spokespersons—to construct a proper discourse on issues of race, identity, and class has been the primary impediment to developing and sustaining a movement for social change in the United States. Without such movement(s) the trajectory of U.S. foreign policy from constructive engagement (covert operations that recognize the public's disapproval) to unilateralism (an open triumphlist nationalism that actually mobilizes the majority public behind its imperialist aggression, Democratic fascism) shouldn't be surprising. The manner in which crime laws and legislation promoting prison growth have been enacted by elected representatives while social services, education spending for public schools, and the future prospects for Social Security spending have dwindled significantly is the logical outcome of a weakened African American intellectual base; the lack of post-civil rights leadership response to the increasing significance of whiteness.

MULTIRACIALISM

The terrible toll antiblack racism takes on individuals on a daily basis can be measured in many different degrees, but as history has shown, anyone with any suspicion of melanin runs the risk of incurring empire's iron fists of racism. More significantly, most African Americans are subjected to some form of repression simply for being poor. Harsh and punitive government repression in the form of prisons, racial profiling, and day-to-day psychological assaults, workplace discrimination, and prejudice serve as uninterrupted legacies of racial slavery; harsh reminders that white supremacy is in a regenerative rather than degenerative stage of its development. Having outlived plantation slavery, Jim Crow, and apartheid, racism has become a lived experience among virtually all African Americans. Yet, more prevalent, more globalized than ever before, it can now be brushed underneath the carpet, concealed behind the veil of "progress" and postmodernization.

This much is apparent to any conscious person of African descent, and increasingly, some awareness is being generated among Arab and Southeast Asian immigrants, as their civil rights vanish in the age of 9/11. Such conditions make the prospects of renewed black protests inevitable, even as the form in which it will ultimately express itself becomes increasingly unpredictable. It is this possibility that causes the ruling strata of society so much anxiety. What is to be done? This remains the burning question of the hour. But there are new factors to consider before proceeding along the road to freedom blindly and chaotically.

Today, as so-called identity movements[73] of various types have made it clear, the "others" must be recognized, and this recognition must be expanded much further beyond token celebrations of our diversity: Multiculturalism will not suffice! The simultaneity of these two developments—the rising tide of historical consciousness and identity politicization among various "minority" groups (or groups defined as other) on the one hand, and the increasingly repressive regime of white supremacy (this repression is accompanied by a new surge of nativism, racism, and imperialism) on the other—constitutes, perhaps, the most monumental conflict in contemporary America. How has this development altered the course of black visions of freedom?

Do new "racial" demographics complicate discourse on race, ethnicity, and national identity? While it is true that race relations can no longer be discussed in black/white binary terminology that ignores the presence of other nonblack people of color, does this also mean that antiblack racism has disappeared?

Prior to the so-called age of exploration, Native Americans primarily inhabited the New World. Then between the fifteenth and early twentieth centuries, there was a massive transfer of people to the Western Hemisphere; from Africa, the European mainland, and the Anglo Celtic offshore islands of Europe. Although Chinese and Filipinos reached Mexico on the ships of the Manila galleon as early as the 1600s, their migration to North America generally corresponded with westward expansion, particularly when gold was discovered in California in 1848. A large number of British, Germans, and Irish began to immigrate to the United States around the 1830s. After the Civil War, Scandinavians and Eastern and Southern Europeans began to stream in, as well as a small number of Middle Easterners, Japanese, and a second wave of Chinese. Between the late 1950s to the present, South Asians began to enter as a new source of technically skilled labor.

Today, there are also a considerable number of a people traditionally considered African American or black who when given a chance to indicate more than one racial or ethnic identity on the census have chosen to do so. In addition, there are significant numbers of Africans who have migrated to the New World after the period of state-sponsored segregation, unburdened by the psychological restraints of slavery— so they pretend. Instead of identifying themselves as Africans in America, or Africans, many have come up with new identities like Nigerian American, Ethiopian American, and so on, further complicating the pan-African project.

America is clearly one of the most racially plural countries in the world, and a number of scholars and educators have advocated multiculturalism, a perspective that is more inclusive of "otherness," as a response to this growing tide and as an alternative to the discredited concept of Eurocentrism. In reality, though, most of these advocates champion multiculturalism as a way of safeguarding the status quo from other more autonomous cultural identities that have surfaced over the past three decades.

Given the logic of racial capitalism, one would reason that nonblack people of color would be more united with African Americans in the sphere of politics, but no such alliances appear on the horizon; instead, various racial groups have competed with one another for what they consider to be their slice of the pie. One noticeable exception to this rule is when the bourgeois strata of these groups coalesce for economic reasons; for example, at local government levels where they are encouraged to work together to ensure themselves a stake in the sometimes lucrative business of obtaining minority contracts, or to carry out their duties as buffers between the elite families and the poor. It is here, behind the curtains, where we witness strange bedfellows in action.

AFRICAN AMERICANS AND PEOPLE OF COLOR

Generally speaking, however, these immigrants—as individuals—gravitate more toward groupthink on the subject of race relations. They might have an abstract appreciation of King's "I Have a Dream" speech, but are not likely to identify with the radical struggles of black people, as their ideological orientations are usually procapitalist, and certainly anticommunist. Immigrant activists, unlike the young black radicals whom they are likely to encounter while having tea, are likely to have been privileged with two or three African American studies courses, and thus have an indispensable knowledge base from which to draw when discussing black politics; have listened to rap music and thus experienced blackness. Those immigrants born in America between the years 1970 and 1984, no doubt, seem to identify with an imagined hip-hop community, and enough have participated in various anarchist formations to now begin the process of reformulating their own "people of color" collectives that promise to maintain the same racial hierarchies as their parent organizations. Their main concern is the need for increased political space, which they mistakenly believe African Americans have monopolized.

Young black activists, however, are in urgent need of clarity regarding who their global allies are, for they might find themselves in bed with strange fellows at a critical moment in history. For example, one El Salvadorian "person of color" in Houston informed me, emphasizing—perhaps bragging—about her class identity, "My father played poker with the gentlemen in charge of the death squads." But I am in solidarity with the peasants of El Salvador, I responded.

In San Francisco a young Palestinian woman, just having returned home from a trip to the West Bank, shared her feelings about how fortunate *we* are, how *we* take the freedom *we* have in this country for granted; how she appreciated being back home in this regard. While she identified herself as antiwar and progressive, she voiced opposition to the recognized Palestinian leadership in which her family played a prominent part. She was very opposed to the idea of Palestinian statehood and criticized those Palestinians engaged in war with the Israeli army. Like many in her generation (she was in her twenties), she rejects the two-state solution in favor of the idea of binationality, a situation that would join together the West Bank, Gaza, and Israel to form a secular state where Jews and Palestinians would have equal rights under the law. But I told her that I am for Palestinian self-determination and in my heart stand with her brothers and sisters who are fighting against the settlers, Mossad and Israeli Defense Force in self-defense.

From what I have experienced in my meetings with the younger generation of Left "people of color" formations, their ideas about social change are often incompatible with the aims and goals of those struggling against a global system of racial capitalism. Sure, they have grievances that are as legitimate as those of African Americans, but most believe that African American politics occupies too much space, and they are overly preoccupied with making sure such space is minimized. While African American public intellectuals, usually far-removed from electoral and grassroots politics, espouse multiracial and class movements in their various texts, their "expertise" on these issues rarely stems from actually having worked within multiracial alliances. Most often their theory lacks any personal ties to praxis. Terms like "poor whites" regularly show up in their polemical work, but I have been in meetings, conferences, and alliances with poor whites and have rarely, if ever, seen an African American *public* intellectual involved in such organizational formations. Yet it is within such inconspicuous organizational spaces and among people committed to social change that their critical engagement is most needed—and their disengagement reflects a larger crisis in public intellectualism.

RACE, POLITICALLY AND HISTORICALLY SPEAKING

Interestingly, many of these academics appear to latch on to highly commoditized theoretical fashions far more quickly than the "masses" they claim are permeably "locked down" by the capitalist market. For instance, the recent media attention given to human genome research has led to a preoccupation among academicians, cultural critics and politicians (former U.S. president Bill Clinton heralded the findings as one of the most important events of the twentieth century) with the concept of race as a social construction. This research only confirms what some have argued for centuries: Human beings are part of the same biological family. In theory, this concept is admirable and signals a major departure from Lothrop Stoddard's *The Rising Tide of Color* (1923)[74] and Madison Grant's *The Passing of a Great Race* (1916).[75] It appears to offer a rebuttal to the more contemporary Jared Taylors[76] and J. Phillippe Rushtons of the world who argue African American inferiority and innate predisposition to criminal activity. Aside from rhetoric, however, the human genome research has little to offer in regard to forestalling or putting an end to the intensification of racism, and provides no foreseeable policy being implemented by the federal government to curtail antiblack violence. In fact, if we look beyond the intellectual discourse on this subject being constructed by historians and pay closer attention to what the geneticists are arguing, we can assume that eventually—sooner than later—racial determinists will finally conceive of the scientific heresy to assert that innate differences are written into our genes, biologically inherited; and, alas, thus explains the racial hierarchy of society among other more dangerous concerns.

Yet when African Americans attempt to organize around color in response to antiblack racism, they are often accused of reverse racism, urged to abandon identity politics (as if identity politics is on an equal footing with racism) and are told race is a social construct (and while I'm only speculating, I can't imagine that other racial and ethnic groups are told the same thing). In the United States, in exchange for scientific explanations, racism is simply practiced—a much more advantageous and economical way of administering racial repression.

The response of the establishment commentators to the increasing identity politicization has been to suggest that race is a social construction, setting up straw arguments with "extremists" as if anyone with a modicum of intelligence believes in racial purity. Yet even this supposedly enlightened idea hasn't had any bearing on the political and social reality of race relations in America, and thus, the credibility it warrants—not necessarily from the various anthropologists, social scientists, or geneticists who propose it, but from those who use it to defend racism—appears terribly disingenuous.

More than anything, in America race has been a historical construction and the forecast of empire's troubled history of race diminishing are ill conceived. Sadly, James Baldwin's 1963 comment on race—that color was a political reality—is truer now than when he said it.[77] His point becomes quite evident when one witnesses the current response to the rising tide of historical and cultural awakening among various ethnic groups of color, a response particularly noticeable among, but not limited to, the right wing. At the twilight of the twenty-first century, racism has reentered through the front door of mainstream society without as much as knocking, while progressives anticipate its arrival through the back door.

It is predicted that by 2050, the breakdown of racial groups by percentage will be as such: European Americans, 52.8 percent; African Americans, 13.2 percent; Hispanic Americans, 24.3 percent; Asian Americans, 8.9 percent; and Native Americans, 0.8 percent. But according to George Yancey's study, *Who Is White: Latinos, Asians, and the New Black/NonBlack Divide*, the predictions that whites will become a minority are misleading because the definition of who is white will include Asians and Latinos.[78] There are no such predictions about the declining significance of race, however. The historical construct of race, in all of its antiblack manifestations, will continue to pervade global life. In the international scenario racial nativism is on the rise throughout Western Europe.

LIBERAL ANTIBLACK DISCOURSE

For sure, the successes of a highly organized minority right wing is largely to blame for the present expressions of antiblack racism and deserves serious attention, but Arthur M. Schlesinger, Jr., for instance, isn't exactly the militia type. In his "national bestseller," *The Disuniting of America*,[79] Schlesinger makes several arguments that amount to an overreaching attack against the growing cultural awareness and identity politicization among the various non-Anglo populations, and special consideration is given to African Americans. More specifically, his harshest criticisms are reserved for the Afrocentrists, whom he feels pose a grave threat to empire's liberal project.

In a strong sense, Schlesinger is suggesting that African Americans forget their African past. He echoes Hector St. John de Crèvecoeur's sense of what constitutes an American[80]:

> In a nation marked by an even stranger mixture of blood than Crèvecoeur had known, his celebrated question is asked once more, with a new passion— and a new answer. Today many Americans disavow the historic goal of "a new race of man." The escape from origins yields to the search for roots. The "ancient prejudices and manners" disowned by Crèvecoeur have made a surprising comeback. A cult of ethnicity has arisen both among nonAnglo whites and among nonwhite minorities to denounce the idea of a melting pot, to challenge the concept of "one people," and to protect, promote, and perpetu- ate separate ethnic and racial communities.[81]

Schlesinger is lamenting the demise of empire's melting pot, where all arriving subjects were expected to forget their past; in other words, leave their baggage behind, and assimilate. All were

expected to do this except, of course, certain Anglo Americans.
Schlesinger acknowledges that the melting pot didn't melt everyone, including some Anglo Americans. But when he addresses
the issues of enslavement and genocide of Africans and Native
Americans, his choice of words reek of indifference:

> Those long in America whom the European newcom-
> ers overran and massacred, or those others hauled in
> against their will from Africa and Asia—deeply bred
> racism put them all, red Americans, black Americans,
> yellow Americans, brown Americans, well outside
> the pale. The curse of racism was the great failure of
> the American ideals and the still crippling disease of
> American life.[82]

To suggest that the holocaust of Native Americans and the
enslavement of Africans was "the great failure of the American ideals" is quite remarkable, for few acts in the history of
modern humanity have been more deliberately orchestrated, so
systematically perpetrated. While acknowledging that Africans
were brought to America against their will he implies that they
might not be the best suited to determine their destinies. After
all, throughout the book he bends over backward to instruct
African American intellectuals who have dared to think beyond
the pot.

Throughout *The Disuniting* whiteness is legitimated, as he
essentially argues in Eurocentric terms:

> Martin Luther King Jr. did pretty well with Thoreau,
> Gandhi, and Reinhold Niebuhr as models—remem-
> ber, after all, whom King (and his father) were named
> for. The record hardly shows that "Eurocentric"
> education had such a terribly damaging effect on
> the psyche of great black Americans. Why deny it to
> black children today? Why not dwell with DuBois
> above the veil? Is Lincoln to be a hero only for those
> of English ancestry? Jackson only for Scotch-Irish?
> Douglass only for blacks? Great artists, thinkers,

leaders are the possessions not just of their own racial clan but of all humanity.[83]

Read again: Everyone should rally around Eurocentrism, for after all it hasn't been a bad modernist project. One wonders whether Schlesinger is attempting to change careers from historian to comedian. It is as if he believes that during the peopling of American empire, Africans and Native Americans were nowhere around. As Molefi K. Asante notes in his appropriate response to the book, "Schlesinger sets forth a vision of the United States of America rooted in the past where Anglo-Saxon whites defined the protocols of the American society and white culture itself represented the example to which others were forced to aspire."[84] Of course Schlesinger is hardly alone in this regard.

COMING TO AMERICA

An extensive body of literature from a wide range of perspectives disputes such thinking on Schlesinger's part.[85] Colin A. Palmer notes in his book, *Passageways*:

> [Africans] were not immigrants in search of a better life. They were property. But Africans were more than just property. As human beings, they brought with them their culture, ideas, and worldviews; these were the ingredients for preserving linkages with their ancestral homelands. Thus the slave trade represented more than the forced transportation of peoples; Africa came to America as well. The journey was marked by a profound anguish, pain, and suffering, and a remarkable human and cultural resilience as well. These would remain in large measure, and for a long time, the defining characteristics of black life in America.[86]

And *came to America* they did. Joseph E. Inikori and Stanley L. Engerman, in the introduction to their anthology *The Atlantic Slave Trade*, remind us that between 1500 and 1800 more Africans than Europeans arrived in the Americas, and "for the first time in the history of the world, immense opportunities for the development of a division of labor across diverse regions of the world, all linked together by the Atlantic Ocean" took shape.[87] There is, they argue, sufficient enough evidence to suggest that no two groups stand more central to the economic and cultural development of the Western Hemisphere than the African and Native Americans.

Too often we conceive of the present structure of capitalism as if it developed separate and apart from slavery, when in fact enough has been learned to now assume in our discourse that capitalism itself owes its vital components to the economic system established by the architects of the Atlantic complex. Of course this was in no way voluntary, and despite the integral part Africans played in shaping the New World economy, since their arrival every immigrant group in the United States (including those of non-European descent) have appeared to surpass them as far as economics are concerned.

The successes of these "model minority"[88] groups, in fact, have made African American conditions appear to be a result of their own unique failings rather than the systematic structural constraints levied against them, as well as their history of slavery and genocide in this country. In addition, it fosters antiblackness among various immigrants of color. If one adheres to the national mythology that continues to shape public discourse, they would reason that the Middle Passage was simply a free ride; at best a singular and momentary catastrophe to be gotten over with time rather than a prolonged regenerating system of social death. Jim Crow, prisons, and the Federal Bureau of Investigation's (FBI) Counterintelligence Program (COINTELPRO) were altogether insignificant in the undermining of African American modernist project. Conservative intellectuals (for lack of a better term) like Dinesh D'Souza, Thomas Sowell, Walter Williams, and some who are lesser-known have endured themselves to the extreme Right for their excessive commentary regarding African American crises because they have argued as such.

Williams, in his book *The State Against Blacks*, suggests that the principal enemy of African American development is state involvement, and that racism can't possibly be the reason for the problems African Americans face: "Clearly, the experience of Orientals, Jews, and West Indians calls into question the hypothesis that racial bigotry can be a complete explanation of the difficulties that blacks face in America."[89] Conservatives like Williams are always on standby to perform damage control for reactionary policies implemented by congressional lawmakers. Fox television commentator and journalist Armstrong Williams, for example, regularly defends the actions of George W. Bush, and has even served as an apologist for the late racist, segregationist Strom Thurmond (his former employer) on regular occasion. Of course, Williams gets paid, $215,000, in fact, to help promote Bush's "No Child Left Behind" law.[90] Such political minstrelsy is in high demand, and as such, individuals like Williams have gained fame and fortune for trivializing the grievances of the victims: "The Irish were discriminated against; how did they strive and advance in American empire? The Jews suffered a holocaust, how did they make it? The Caribbean people have done well economically and they're black," they argue in an outrageously dreadful chorus. "Quit playing the race card; quit playing the victim." In the end, appropriate and humane responses to antiblack discrimination and racism are dismissed as attempts to "get over."[91]

I was unfortunate enough to catch the last few minutes of a lecture Walter Williams was presenting to a group of conservative youth aired on C-SPAN television. As Williams came to his conclusion, the camera panned the entire room, which was, as far as I could tell, predominately comprised of young white males and perhaps two or three Asians who blended in; at about this point, he was wrapping up his speech and the question and answer session got under way. A young, seemingly nervous white man, after awkwardly putting his words together, finally got to the heart of his question: Should African Americans receive reparations or compensation for past injustices?

For a brief moment—before the sound of his voice had taken effect—I had a feeling of empathy with Walter Williams because I have been in similar situations during lectures I have presented to young people across the country. Shortly after September 11, 2001, I gave a lecture titled "African American Politics in the Age of 9/11" to a group of mostly white students, and a member of the audience asked me a very similar question, the difference being I was and am not altogether sure whether he was a proponent of reparations. He probably asked because I had mentioned in my speech how the events of 9/11 eclipsed the issues of reparations and voting rights violations, as well as other issues like the pacifist protests against the World Trade Organization/International Monetary Fund taking place throughout the world. More specifically, I was simply highlighting how important the issue of slavery was, as demonstrated by the centrality it held in the discourse at the United Nations Conference against World Racism in Durban, South Africa. I suggested that had 9/11 not occurred, the central issue in American politics would probably have been that of slavery and reparations. Thus, considering my own experience, it might be a grave mistake to simply assume the young man who posed the question to Williams was against the idea. He, too, was probably interested in gaining some insight that would allow him to further explore the idea. I ended my response by saying that, if nothing else, the reparations movement would create the context for some type of much-needed public discourse on the issue; a lot of positive results would come out of that discussion. It is certain, however, that Williams did whatever he could to alleviate any possibilities of him pursuing the issue any further.

I cannot quote him verbatim, except to say that he referred to the reparations movement as bull dung, to put it nicely. He then suggested the young man visit his Website, which includes a proclamation of amnesty and pardon for white Americans. I paid the Website a visit:

> Whereas, Europeans kept my forebears in bondage
> some three centuries toiling without pay,

Whereas, Europeans ignored the human rights pledges of the Declaration of Independence and the United States Constitution,

Whereas, the Emancipation Proclamation, the Thirteenth and Fourteenth Amendments meant little more than empty words,

Therefore, Americans of European ancestry are guilty of great crimes against my ancestors and their progeny.

But, in the recognition Europeans themselves have been victims of various and sundry human rights violations to wit: the Norman Conquest, the Irish Potato Famine, Decline of the Hapsburg Dynasty, Napoleonic and Czarist adventurism, and gratuitous insults and speculations about the intelligence of Europeans of Polish descent,

I, Walter E. Williams, do declare full and general amnesty and pardon to all persons of European ancestry, for both their own grievances, and those of their forbearers, against my people.

Therefore, from this day forward Americans of European ancestry can stand straight and proud knowing they are without guilt and thus obliged not to act like damn fools in their relationships with Americans of African ancestry.[92]

Not being a psychiatrist, I am not prepared to discuss the psychosis apparently inflicting individuals like Williams, except to suggest that his case provides a compelling argument for compensation—compensation for the illness of slavery mentality.

Nor, however, am I unaware that a number of other ethnic and religious groups, including some now considered white and "mainstream," (i.e., Jews, Irish, Catholics, Mormons, et al.) have had their *experiences*. All one has to do is read John Higham's *Strangers in the Land: Patterns of American Nativism, 1860-*

1925.[93] In his book the word *Strangers* is in no way meant to imply African Americans. Rather Higham goes into great detail examining the history of nativism on American soil, revealing much about intra-European prejudices. But none of the groups vaguely mentioned above have had to endure slavery, racial discrimination of the sort that blacks have experienced, and until recently (9/11), none besides Hispanics have endured the constraints of systemic racial profiling, a process of policing that has wreaked havoc within the black communities. Much is made of the migration of indentured servants, yet "Indentured servitude offered the passport of freedom," writes Betty Wood in her book *The Origins of American Slavery*. It offered "the prospect of land ownership, and the possibility of a potentially unlimited upward mobility."[94]

Above all, in their journey toward whiteness they have been allowed to *forget* not only the identity they left behind across the Atlantic, but also the oppression they have suffered in this country. Talk to young Irish, Jew and other non-Anglo whites about their history of discrimination and one will either discover a remarkable sense of forgetfulness or deafening silence on the part of most.

Years ago, I took part in an American history seminar that focused on the period of the Gilded Age and Progressive Era. During one discussion, the instructor, who was an Irishman, provided a list of the wealthiest individuals of this period. After some discussion, he posed a question to the group of students, most of whom were Catholic: Why weren't any Catholics among this group? There was a self-assured silence, and I am convinced it wasn't because of embarrassment, but more likely because of their collective sense of self-identity, as well as, perhaps, their journey towards whiteness. A little less than half were of Irish descent, one of the numerous ethnic groups to have had its *experience*. While the prospects of entrepreneurial success were promising to immigrants, not all were immediately welcomed into the melting pot. This was certainly true of Irish and Catholics, as indicated by their conspicuous absence within the ranks of the business elite. But they eventually melted; a Kennedy finally became President and Reagan soon followed. The Daley machine remains intact in Chicago.

African Americans, despite their struggles for acceptance, have never been successful in erasing the stigma of race. How could they? Where do we start? Middle Passage? Slavery? Reconstruction? Black Codes? Tuskegee Experiment? Birmingham? Inglewood? Simi Valley? O.J. Simpson? Prison Industrial Complex? Housing Discrimination? "What Does Jesse Want?" Katrina? African Americans are constantly reminded of their race and place in society. While the European ethnic immigrants from across the Atlantic were eventually granted their "white" cards, African Africans have had to make due with the "race" card.[95] For *Blacks* the melting pot narrative has obviously outlived itself, and the race card, as recent events have demonstrated, has expired.[96] Is there a light at the end of the tunnel? Yes, perhaps, but as one friend of mine puts it, "It may not be the light I envisioned."

In the present climate of 9/11 many have begun to reassess what it means to be patriotic, to be American. Not surprisingly, *black* (i.e., African American) continues to serve as trope for "criminal, problem, subversive, unworthy, and un-American" while "others" (i.e., foreign people of color), so long as they act in accordance with the status quo, are accepted (or they are at least allowed to think they are) as Americans, just as long as they're not *too* Muslim. This privilege is extended to include select African Americans as well, but the cost for them is usually greater. Even within the context of the "War on Terrorism," one has to be very alarmed, for beneath the banner of "United We Stand," the "blacklash" continues.

Racist thinking and political behavior continue in more subtle forms, even among the Left, and I am certain it has to do with a lack of historical and overall social consciousness among the new breed of activists, as well as the inability of the Old Left (regarded as the New Left) to overcome the political immaturity and racial sectarianism that grew out of the 1960s in response to the black power and various other identity movements. So consumed with or by whiteness, the left have frowned upon challenges to the "master narrative."

AMERICAN REALITY

Social movements do not occur in a vacuum. They coincide with, visibly confront, or evolve alongside opposite political and social forces. This has been true of all antiracist movements within the United States. Antiracism has been confronted with the increasing significance of whiteness (a grand experiment of sorts) and an attempt by empire's intellectual apparatus to solidify a monolithic outlook among white ethnic immigrant groups from across the Atlantic (and Pacific). To a large extent, this experiment has succeeded. Whiteness is now embedded within both the institutional structures and the hegemonic superstructure of racial empire. The prospect of this trend reversing itself doesn't look promising, for such movement against racial empire has been cast as reverse racism and unpatriotic.

This is perhaps the moment to turn our attention toward a lecture given by C.L.R. James, the Trinidadian Marxist whose political thought is widely referenced within New Left scholarship. In the speech, James is attempting to come to terms with the burgeoning movement among black students for Black studies programs in the United States. In his manner of thinking, one's conception of Western history was limited if it didn't come with an understanding of the role Africans played in the North's victory during the Civil War.

According to James, President Abraham Lincoln's conception of nationality wasn't based on color but experience, specifically the experience of achieving the American Revolution. "Lincoln implied that there were no such people in other parts of the world because none of them had that great experience," James told the audience.

> Then he went on to say, what about those people who
> have come from foreign countries and come to the
> United States, the Germans in particular? He said
> the Declaration of Independence and what it states
> and the experience of living alongside those people
> who were descendants of those who had fought in
> the War of Independence—that was making the
> Germans into citizens worthy of being members of
> the great American Republic.[97]

James goes on to suggest that it wasn't until the Africans had
taken up arms and helped save the day during the Civil War that
Lincoln changed his mind.

James could appreciate Lincoln's conception, for although
perhaps in a different vein as W.E.B. DuBois, he linked citizenship to military service. Military service, of course, was in practical terms synonymous with patriotism and, I would add, imperialism. DuBois, for example, would test this logic in his infamous
"Close Ranks" editorial in July 1918, which argued that blacks
should forego their struggle for civil rights and social equality
for the good of the country: "Let us not hesitate. Let us, while
this war lasts, forget our special grievances and close our ranks
shoulder to shoulder with our white fellow citizens and the allied
nations that are fighting for democracy." Notwithstanding the
probability that it was an attempt to sell his people out for the
rank of captain in the Military Intelligence and the benefits that
would accrue from such a venture, I'm willing to give DuBois the
benefit of the doubt when he suggested that at no time had he
felt more American.[98] Referring to Lincoln, James notes:

> He changed his mind when he saw the black people
> fighting in the war; he felt that they, just as the people
> who had fought in the War of Independence, were
> now proving that they were perfectly able to be citi-
> zens of the Republic in the tradition which had been
> established by the men who had fought in the War of
> Independence.[99]

James's apology for Lincoln's ignorance vaguely contradicts the real narrative of the history of black struggle and its broader significance in legitimating the idea of a multiracial democracy. Because much of what America supposedly stands for, or, put another way, what it means to be an American, is tied to the foundational period of the American Revolution, we must began to seriously rethink the primary role blacks have played in progressive and revolutionary movements throughout this country's history, and I do not mention the word "revolution" uneasily.

I would like to suggest that African American struggles for citizenship rights (abolition, civil rights, reparations, etc.) comprise the most powerful and enduring force toward defining American citizenship; ironically this definition of a citizenship has yet to be extended to them in full. African American movements have played a central role in defining the character of social change in American society, as far back as the American Revolution.

In their very significant book, *The Many-Headed Hydra*, Peter Linebaugh and Marcus Rediker, for example, strongly suggest that it was a motley crew of sailors, slaves, laborers, pirates, indentured servants, and market women whose ideas of freedom and equality laid the basis for the revolutionary impulses of 1776. Not only did this group shape "[the] organizational history of the American Revolution[it had] an even greater impact upon its intellectual history, influencing the ideas of Samuel Adams, J. Philmore, James Otis, Jr., Anthony Benezet, Thomas Paine, and John Allen."[100]

But every antiracist movement in America, beginning with the early abolitionist movement preceding the American Revolution, which called for the emancipation of the enslaved Africans, to the present movement around the issue of reparations for individuals of African descent, have been cast in an un-American light. And too often, the Left has fallen for this pretext, opposing such movements simply because it has been too immersed in its own sense of whiteness to comprehend the broader implications.

I doubt this political behavior will ever change. These contradictions will remain as invisible to those who view themselves as beneficiaries of the system as they are unmistakably clear to those who reside on the margins.

For blacks, their prospects of being included as citizens have always been overpriced and unattainable. For no matter what Lincoln said in that speech or letter, his actions during the Civil War were taken as war measures, and at the war's conclusion, the conditions of Africans remained the same, just as they had at the conclusion of the Revolution and all the other imperial wars thereafter. For the immigrant, his and her price was simply to become *white*. Perhaps using the word *simply* diminishes the sacrifices that go together with one's journey toward whiteness, living alongside the descendents of the founding fathers and having to learn how to be a citizen.

The United States has become metonymic of racial empire. The twisting and often illusory trajectory of social and political reform in America has been defined as progress, yet some are asking: Are we at the end of history? Has it come to racial empire, where whiteness becomes an invisible source of power, periodically raising its head to remind "them" of their place at the bottom? Will the erosion of civil liberties, mass imprisonments, military tribunals, presidential takeovers, and internment camps become the defining characteristics of twenty-first century empire?

Anne D. Neal and Jerry Martin, in their report, *Defending Civilization: How Our Universities Are Failing America and What Can Be Done About It*, suggest that universities failed America by not passing on the values of freedom and democracy.[101] They chide professors for refusing to endorse air strikes that kill more innocent bystanders than enemy combatants. They lambaste the liberal-minded intelligentsia for not being vocal enough in articulating their patriotism, and, in many instances, for pointing the finger at American foreign policy as contributing to the climate of terrorism. In addition, they evoke the spirit of the late David Bloom's *Closing of the American Mind*,[102] chiding the universities for rushing to add courses on Islamic and Asian courses while being less stringent in their requirements of students to take surveys of Western civilization. Compiling a list of more than 100 names and quotes—in a sense reinventing McCarthyism—they argue for a return to the past and a collective rememorization:

> America's first line of defense is a confident under-standing of how and why this nation was founded, and the continuing relevance and urgency of its first principles. It depends on its intellectuals both for its philosophical defense and for passing its heritage on to the next generation....We learn from history that when a nation's intellectuals are unwilling to defend its civilization, they give aid and comfort to its adver-saries.[103]

One wonders whether Neal and Martin are fully conscious of their argument, or whether they're looking in the mirror in search of adversaries. In any event, the above quote exemplifies the role they feel intellectuals should play in social life. "That is not patriotism, but fascism," argues Roberto J. Gonzalez, an assistant professor in the Department of Anthropology at San Jose State University, in response to the report. "The American Council's position is inaccurate and irresponsible. Critique, debate, and exchange—not blind consensus or self censorship—have charac-terized America since its inception."[104] Wrong!

Fascism has existed under the guise of racism for decades, and only now has it become slightly less discriminating—that is all. In the context of "the war on terrorism" the criminalization of dissent has been made visible to most. And thus the old adage, "When in Rome, do as Romans do," has once again become the mantra of the Left, who are on one hand now frightened by the intensified censorship and, on the other, opportunistic enough to take full advantage of the spoils. The wages of whiteness are much greater than we have been led to believe.

I suppose strange times make for strange bedfellows because I'm in much agreement with Lynne Cheney, the vice president's wife, who is quoted by Martin and Neal as saying students need to "know the ideas and ideals on which our nation has been built"[105] but not for the reasons she would give. In truth, America has little history of social progress it can take credit for, unless, of course, we include the struggles of those who have come before: The resistance of enslaved Africans, the abolitionists movements, the civil rights and black power movements, Chicano power, women's movements, and others whose movements, when taken as a whole, have been a humanizing and civilizing force. And rarely has progress been made without suspicious demands. In fact, the enduring presence of such racial suspicion presents the most compelling reason why a radical redefinition of values and an abolition of whiteness, accompanied by the abolition of institutional and economic structures that perpetuate racism, will be central to formulating any agenda for real social change both domestically and globally.

I must admit that there are times when I find myself growing grim about that romanticized day when the Left will change the face of its political activity, but history has shown this change to be unlikely. I do not intend to make a blanket indictment against the Left because some marginalized efforts as described above are already under way, and history has shown that what occurs along the margins oftentimes has the greater impact on the center. However, there is more than enough reason to be alarmed.

The move toward whiteness, particularly from the Left, gives me much to worry about.[106] It seems the attention of liberal cultural critics and public intellectuals, particularly since the end of the Cold War, has been focused solely on discrediting struggles led by African Americans, whose struggles usually revolve around issues that have an immediate and unbearable impact on their tenuous daily existence in America. Yet the "culture of complaint" that brought about hate crimes legislation, and the contestations against racial profiling that at least halted its excesses, provide part of the basis upon which the present fight against the erosion of civil liberties can proceed.

It is quite possible that a straightforward dialogue on race relations in the United States—the likelihood of this ever occurring—has become an increasing impossibility given the present circumstances. Perhaps this is the most compelling reason for the indomitable silence we now witness on the part of African American leadership regarding the various crises confronting their communities. Of course one can only bear witness to what one has seen or perhaps heard, thus I would hesitate to suggest that there have been no rumblings from below, no resistance from those who are already bearing the brunt of empire's repression—the weight of it's collapse—both at home and abroad, whose struggles are marginalized by both empire and their intellectual gatekeepers. There certainly are such voices. But without an organized movement, these voices are not likely to be heard enough, and is there any guarantee what they have to say will be much different from those cast as leaders by the establishment?

CONCLUSION

I have touched upon a wide range of issues, both historical and contemporary, which I feel are all interconnected at the present historical moment. They warrant serious attention on the part of those who yearn to realize an alternative vision of the world apart from that put forth by the present world leadership. How we see our past often determines the manner in which we struggle for our future, hence I have taken a sweeping view of African American history: from the period of abolition, with particular emphasis on the life and career of Frederick Douglass; to a general critique of the present discourse generated by the likes of liberal academic William Julius Wilson, and the political behavior exhibited by political figures such as Vernon Jordan. But, even as my discussion has been profoundly interdisciplinary, it remains compartmentalized. As I mentioned earlier, Frederick Douglass could have chosen to interrogate the issue of race and architecture, literature, religion, and language—he was well aware of the events around him. What would he have to say about popular sports, new forms of modern media, and the ways in which they impact on race and identity in America? And what would he have made of the antiblack racism exhibited by non-African people of color? Would Douglass choose to speak on the Fourth of July?

African American intellectuals have a tremendous role to play in America's future. America is the place where the vast majority of African Americans will call home both now and in the foreseeable future. Given this reality, they must seriously consider engaging a new set of assumptions regarding history, economics, and culture. And honestly engaging the centrality of whiteness and antiblackness in left politics will be a good, indeed necessary, starting point.

No longer can we simply look at racism as a power relationship between whites and blacks. Serious thought must be given to the manner in which new immigrants have subscribed to the logic of antiblackness in ways that are perhaps more complicated than the traditional forms of white supremacy. If indeed our struggle must reflect the world we wish to build, then we are at a vexing crossroad. For one, I am not willing to struggle for a world where the present ideological structures of whiteness remain intact.

Where do we go from here? I believe we must simply continue in the tradition symbolized by the heroic struggles of such prophetic voices of resistance as Frederick Douglass, Marcus Garvey, Malcolm X, Harriet Tubman, Sojourner Truth, Ernesto "Che" Guevara, Walter Rodney, Martin Luther King, Jr.—individuals (too numerous to mention all of them) *honestly* responding to the events around them.

A study of history reveals that without struggle, there will be no progress. It reveals that without demands, justice is too slow to come, and perhaps more pointedly, the contradictions of racial inequality will be made increasingly difficult for young Americans to discern. For this reason, black leaders will have to speak to the immediacy of black concerns without necessarily offending other groups, but not in the manner William Julius Wilson suggests in *The Bridge Over the Racial Divide*,[107] where black leaders are urged to articulate their problems and concerns in a deracialized language; or in Marable's *Beyond Black and White*,[108] where he is essentially argues for a slightly more inclusive form of neoliberal democracy; or Roberto Unger and Cornel West's liberal tract *The Future of American Progressivism: An Initiative for Political and Economic Reform*,[108] which reminds one of Russian intellectual Peter Struve's (1870-1905) brand of conservative liberalism that dismayed the great Russian revolutionary V.I. Lenin and eventually situated Struve against the more radical revolutionaries who ushered in the Russian Revolution.[109]

The towering world systems theorist Immanuel Wallerstein has argued that within the next fifty years, a new world order will emerge out of chaotic social conditions emerging from the structural limitations of the endless accumulation of capital that at present governs the world economy. He refers to these years as a "transformational Timespace."[110] His warning, however, was issued prior to the ushering in of the attack on the American public on September 11, 2001 (and the subsequent War on Terror). To suggest that the empire is on its deathbed doesn't sound as apocalyptic as it once did, in 1998.

Chapter Four

Black Movements Toward Freedom: Mumia Abu-Jamal and Empire's Prisoners of War

I had the Black Panther Party, who did they have?... I am he, and they are me. From death row, this is Mumia Abu-Jamal.

—Mumia Abu-Jamal

I became aware of Abu-Jamal's ordeal only shortly before he was scheduled to be executed on August 17, 1995, but can still vividly recall the urgent sense of immediacy on the part of political activists and anti-death penalty advocates to mobilize thousands in protest. Appeals were made on Abu-Jamal's behalf from throughout the world—from South Africa, Germany, and France to Brazil, Switzerland, and Cuba. German Foreign Minister Klaus Kinkel made a special request to former Pennsylvania Governor (and later the first head of Homeland Security) Tom Ridge to halt the execution. Also, French President Jacques Chirac gave his support to overturn the death penalty against Abu-Jamal. An unprecedented exhibition of unity among intellectuals, artists, and entertainers was shown. Not since the Free Huey P. Newton and Angela Davis campaigns of the 1970s had this type of mobilization taken place on American soil.

Ten days before the date, on August 7, 1995, Abu-Jamal was granted a stay of execution by Judge Albert Sabo, who wanted to "give[Abu-Jamal] more time to complete the appeals process before the execution date in his death penalty case." Pennsylvania's real reluctance to execute Abu-Jamal, however, had everything to do with the fact that hundreds of thousands of his supporters both from within and outside the American empire made it crystal clear that massive civil disobedience would follow suit. Since then, Abu-Jamal has remained one of the most progressive voices on the scene, authoring several groundbreaking books,[1] writing weekly commentary, and, through Noel Hanrahan's Prison Radio Project, regularly providing always insightful radio commentary.

Because of Mumia Abu-Jamal, public attention—above all, that of the American Left—has increasingly been focused on the issues of the death penalty and political imprisonment. With his case the whole panorama of debate around these two issues widened considerably. In the minds of many activists, a few questions emerged to the center of Left political discourse—particularly that within radical black Left circles. First, was empire's domestic criminal justice system a political institution designed to criminalize black people? Second, was the death penalty, a long-standing mechanism of social control, becoming a new machinery of controlling radical dissent? Finally, were there political prisoners and prisoners of war in the United States?

A political prisoner is usually defined as a person incarcerated for actions carried out in support of legitimate struggles for self-determination or for opposing the illegal policies of a government and/or its political subdivisions. The most obvious reason why the American public knows so little about political imprisonment is because the United States government doesn't acknowledge having them within the confines of its borders. Furthermore, it has not and does not recognize any of its policies (i.e., slavery, genocide of indigenous people) as illegal.

The main reason, however, for the public's unawareness is that most American political prisoners are charged with crimes—albeit crimes they did not commit. The criminal charges are used as a subterfuge for discrediting their political activities, neutralizing or destroying their effectiveness as political organizers. Mainstream journalists—individuals whose writings seem to religiously correspond with government lines of policy—nearly always frame their analysis around questions of guilt or innocence as opposed to the possible connections between the politics of the individuals and their incarcerations; mainstream journalists never attempt to connect these dots. Thus, unless the public is politically educated around the issues, they will view these cases as criminal rather than political.

When the issue of political imprisonment or prisoners of war surfaces in mainstream media, it is usually to misdirect public attention to another time and place. In the recent past, public attention would migrate to faraway places like South Africa; for example, there we witnessed Nelson Mandela, after twenty-seven years of imprisonment for his political convictions, emerge as head of state. Or, in the case of prisoners of war, we think of Vietnam veterans like Arizona Senator John McCain or others who were/are missing in action (MIAs). No doubt, with the installations of Abu-Ghraib and Guantanamo Bay prisons—with secret black prisons and torture chambers installed under the guidance of America's CIA placed throughout Europe—few can deny the existence of prisoners of war under the control of American empire.[2] However, the prisoners of war I am referring to in this chapter are located within empire's borders—they are American citizens with names like Leonard Peltier, Sekou Odinga, Geronimo Pratt, Herman Bell, Mohaman Geuka Koti, and Robert Seth Hayes, to name a few. And most important, it is about those who are most likely unknown to the reader. Abu-Jamal is recognized as a political prisoner by human rights activists throughout the world because of his uncompromising journalism, criticism of Philadelphia police brutality, past membership in the Black Panther Party, and his affiliation with the Philadelphia-based MOVE organization during the time of his arrest. Most important, in 1982 he was falsely accused of the murder of Philadelphia police officer Daniel Faulkner—a crime punishable by death. And there are other cases very similar to his occurring wherever empire's dominance is being wielded.

On September 14, 1998, the U.S. House of Representatives passed a congressional resolution calling on the Cuban government to extradite Assata Shakur (her slave name was Joanne Chesimard) with not one dissenting vote. Twenty-three of the Black Congressional Caucus members voted against Assata Shakur while fourteen abstained from voting. Immediately, a well-organized letter writing campaign ensued and the response from one of the leading progressive African American representatives, Maxine Waters (a Democrat representing Watts, California), was that she didn't even know who Assata Shakur was. Whether she was being truthful was beside the point; the real issue was that she and more than twenty others voted to extradite an African American accorded the status of political refugee by the Cuban government—one who fought for the freedom and liberation of African American people—from Cuba to the United States, where she very well could have faced the death penalty.

The bill, co-sponsored by more than twenty congressmen (including former African American Oklahoma representative J.C. Watts and Chicagoan and Puerto Rican representative Luis V. Gutierrez), referred to Chesimard as a "convicted felon" and actually called for the extradition of all the individuals granted political asylum by the Cuban government—a point that seemed to go unnoticed by some. Clearly, the above is just one of numerous examples of the lack of social consciousnesses among African American political leadership, but such political tactlessness contributes a great deal toward much of the public's complacency.

The most striking aspect of Assata Shakur's narrative is that, after not receiving justice in the courts; after being subjected to racialized torture and abuse in the New Jersey prison system, she escaped and managed to make her way to safety. Surely, this is analogous to the preemancipation slave narratives where runaway slaves were one of the most visible threats to the plantation system. Those Africans who managed to escape these brutal plantations served as positive role models for the other enslaved Africans, and, as such, it was incumbent upon the authorities to punish them with the full force of law. At this writing—after nearly three decades—a $1 million bounty has been placed on Shakur by federal authorities. Liberal commentators, as would be expected, ignored the neoslave narrative, instead overwhelmingly choosing to situate these actions within the context of the Venezuelan government's request that the United States extradite Miami Cuban terrorist Luis Pasada Carilles.[3]

Former coordinator of the movement to free Shaka Sankofa, Ashanti Chimurenga, noted that "By looking at how the government was able to criminalize Abu-Jamal's political work, we see an example of what this government was able to do during the period of slavery. The same methods of social control used during the period of slavery—from physical control (attempting to escape from slavery was a crime punishable by death) to the destruction and separation of families—we see in the case of Abu-Jamal."[4] Because of this historical reality, Chimurenga suggested, we should view both political imprisonment and the death penalty from a human rights perspective, as two forms of repressive government practices. The continuity between Slave Codes and the outgrowth of slavery on the part of the government to terrorize and criminalize an entire community of people goes unrecognized by most, thus, we are probably not nearly as terrorized as we should be. Her words certainly apply to the case of Assata Shakur.

Despite the pervasive apathy and unawareness around the issues of the death penalty and political imprisonment, both historically symbolize the most fundamental relationship of power between African American people and the U.S. government apparatus, and the case of Abu-Jamal (indeed, the writings of Mumia himself) helps to clarify such historical linkages.

His importance, however, isn't solely based on the fact that he is facing death at the hand of a racist and criminal body called Pennsylvania, or because he is a politicized proponent of the abolition of legal lynching in America; he is important because he represents the most crystal-clear and eloquent voice of liberation on the contemporary scene. Mumia Abu-Jamal stands squarely in the radical tradition of Nat Turner, Denmark Vesey, John Brown, and so many others who have been persecuted by the state because of their abilities to force the righteousness of their cause into the consciousness of those the state fears most. The American government wishes to silence his voice and neutralize any and all forms of black resistance in the twenty-first century. In very fundamental terms, Mumia Abu-Jamal symbolizes the historical relationship between American empire and its historically subjugated and incarcerated African population.

HISTORICAL BACKDROP OF BMTF

Any discussion of political imprisonment (Mumia Abu-Jamal, the present uses of the death penalty, which, in historical fact, is legalized lynching) has to be done against the historical backdrop of American empire's unrelenting response to what I have called Black Movements Toward Freedom (BMTF). In doing so I believe it will become clear why we must began to expand the definition of political imprisonment so that it is more useful in the present and future stages of our struggle for liberation and freedom. There have been three major movements preceding the present stage of the African American liberation struggle.

First, the Revolutionary War did not, as some historians have suggested, free Africans in the North. Instead, it set in motion a movement toward freedom, and by the turn of the eighteenth century the slave population in the North had gradually given way to a free black population. After the American Revolution various constitutional provisions, state statutes, and court decisions brought about the gradual abolition of slavery: Vermont in 1777, Pennsylvania in 1780, Massachusetts in 1783, Rhode Island in 1784, Connecticut in 1784 and 1797, New York in 1799 and 1812, Ohio in 1802, New Jersey in 1804, Indiana in 1816, and Illinois in 1817.[5] As slavery was progressively abolished in northern states, free Africans gained some mobility, but still their circumstances in civil society were precarious. In addition, the abolition of the slave trade was eventually put into law in 1807, although contraband trade continued to flourish well into the middle part of the nineteenth century, particularly in the Southwest.

Notwithstanding the fact that in most of these states the freedom granted mostly applied to future generations, it marked a turning point in the struggle to abolish slavery. State-sponsored emancipation in the North, as well as the manumission of individuals enslaved Africans in the South, played an important part in creating the material and intellectual space necessary for the development of an educated and politicized leadership who could assist in articulating the aspirations of the masses of enslaved Africans. Eventually this group of free Africans, allied with the left faction of the petite bourgeoisie, would play a significant part in sustaining the Underground Railroad, which in essence was a protracted guerrilla campaign against the southern slave owners.

The founding fathers found the presence of free Africans very disturbing; hence, by 1816 the American Colonization Society (ACS) was formed in an effort to raise funds for the financing and settlement of free Africans in Africa. The eminent historian Frederick Bancroft wrote in 1941:

> It was a slave conspiracy in Virginia in 1800 that prompted the first legislative effort toward colonization, the purpose of which was to eliminate free negroes. Apprehension of uprisings helped to bring the American Colonization Society into existence, in the winter of 1816-17. But as soon as this society manifested vigor and a somewhat antislavery purpose, opposition to it, in the planting regions, increased faster than support. Insisting that it was the free colored population in a slave state, not slavery, that was the great menace, the proslavery men expected to find a sufficient remedy in exiling or enslaving free negroes and dispersing many of the slaves by their sale or removal to the new states and territories.[6]

Historians have differed with one another in their interpretations of events leading up to the ACS's founding, but most agree that the high degree of apprehension resulting from repeated African slave revolts had much to do with encouraging the idea of colonizing free Africans to Africa.

From the beginning, however, free Africans in the North vigorously opposed all forms of colonization and were instrumental in exposing the racist idea as well as urging the white abolitionists to focus more candidly on the issues of slavery, racism, and inequality. Since the idea of forcibly repatriating Africans back to Africa was, among other reasons, seen as too costly, other ways of neutralizing their pursuit of freedom had to be implemented. In her book *Criminalizing a Race*, Charshee Lawrence McIntyre noted that once early attempts at colonization proved too expensive, prisons served as alternative places to removing "free Africans" from society:

> Since the 18th century, the prisons have been the logical holding place for African Americans. Through constantly reinforcing the idea that those of us not in them really represent prime candidates for prisons, these institutions keep us in this society's outsider position. To Whites, blacks not incarcerated simply have not been caught or the prisons lack room to accommodate our entire population. In other words, because Whites have proffered an idea of African American criminality, we have lived for two hundred years in an environment that constantly threatens our freedom.[7]

The ruling class wished to erase the presence of free Africans from the new republic. In 1790, for example, empire's first penitentiary was established in Philadelphia, and McIntyre's well-developed thesis argued that it was primarily created for the purpose of imprisoning the free black population.

Circumstances of the freed Africans in the new empire were such that they were compelled to a more revolutionary disposition toward their enslaved brothers and sisters in the South.

In 1846, an enslaved African named Dred Scott sued in a Missouri court, arguing that he and his family were entitled to their freedom, but in 1857 the United States Supreme Court, 7-2, rejected Scott's claim. Chief Justice Roger Brooke Taney wrote that Africans, even those who were free, should never be considered citizens of the empire, and as such shouldn't be allowed to sue in federal courts. Taney further stated that Congress did not have the power to prohibit slavery in federal territory. This opinion from the highest court in the nation was a harbinger of the Civil War that would soon follow. The Supreme Court essentially ruled that African Americans had no rights that Anglo Americans were bound to respect.[8] Such was the political climate of the times.

Contradictions in the burgeoning capitalist economy eventually reached a point that provided the enslaved Africans with a second major opportunity to make a stride toward freedom. C.L.R. James writes:

> Now one of the things that the industrial capitalists wanted to do was to finish with slavery. It was too expensive. Slave production was backward compared with modern methods and more highly developed capitalist production in agriculture. So that you had on one side the industrial capitalists determined to destroy the slave power of the aristocrats, the commercial capitalists, and the planters. It was in this political struggle that Negroes got their chance to fight for their freedom.[9]

What must be understood by the present generation of activists is that enslaved Africans and those freed Africans in the North, organized, agitated, and rebelled against slavery. Any opportunity to escape from slavery or to advance the movement toward collective freedom was taken advantage of.

However, after the Civil War, many of the formerly enslaved Africans were confronted with conditions nearly as horrendous as chattel slavery, and racial riots increasingly became commonplace in the North. Throughout the South, prisons were constructed to accommodate the newer system of coercing free human labor: convict leasing. The response of the southern oligarchy to their military defeat was to construct more prisons, in many instances not even bothering to move to a new location: Angola in Louisiana, Parchman Farm prison in Mississippi, and others.

"Black codes" were introduced, a plantation-like criminal justice system was established, and increasingly criminologists began constructing a discourse around the inherent criminality of the formerly enslaved African people. Africans, in large numbers, were removed from plantations to prisons; all of this was rationalized by the scientific and scholarly community. In fact, some have questioned whether the Union actually won the war.[10] Despite such overwhelming contradictions, the chimera of Reconstruction undoubtedly ushered in one of the most powerful movements toward freedom.

Jim Crow prevailed until the latter part of the mid-twentieth century, when the civil rights movement began to take shape. During this time, however, the prison industrial complex as we know it today began to grow. Perhaps the most prominent feature of the post-civil rights era has been the growth and expansion of the prison industry established after Reconstruction. This brief synopsis I've presented, if true, should help clarify the primary role of prisons in American empire and thus explain the extraordinary overrepresentation of Africans incarcerated.

I am suggesting that historically prisons have been constructed as institutions of political repression, and their existence depended not primarily on crime but rather upon their efficacy in subduing those deemed troublesome and dangerous to the status quo of racial empire. As noted earlier, the idea of free Africans in the new republic instigated the first reaction; the revolutionary changes in the South brought about by the pyrrhic military victory of the North—yet patent political victory by the South—ushered in the expansion of prisons to regain control of free and cheap labor; and finally, the moral and political assault against Jim Crow brought about the third.

Each of these movements toward freedom, in essence, helped to expand the foundations of the modern idea of democracy. Yet the response to each was to build more prisons and primarily fill them with people of color, specifically African people.

WALLERSTEIN'S PREDICTIONS

At the present historical moment, empire's ruling class faces a dilemma of epic proportions. In his book *Utopistics: Or, Historical Choices of the Twenty-first Century*, Immanuel Wallerstein warns us of a looming period of historical chaos, "hell on earth" as it is. Such catastrophic changes will be brought about because of the structural and historical limitations of capitalism. He predicts a life-and-death struggle between the privileged and those who wish to move empire in an opposite direction for its first time in 500 years.

> The first thing to look at is how those who currently have privilege will react, are indeed reacting. One cannot expect that any significant segment of those who have privilege will relinquish it without struggle, simply on the ground of some appeal to their ethical responsibilities or even to their historical vision. One must assume that they will seek to preserve privilege. Any other presumption is implausible and unrealistic. Even so, we do not know what their strategy will be.

> The optimal strategy by which to defend privilege—the one most likely to be efficacious—has long been a matter of debate among those who hold privilege, and it is not a question upon which social science has offered us any definitive evidence up to now. To start with the simple, there is the division of views between those who believe that repression (at least judicious repression) is the key, and those who believe that concessions that give away a small portion of the pie in order to save the rest are the secret. One can try a mix of both formulas, of course, but then

the question remains, in what proportion and in what sequence?

The fact that historically both methods have been used is not in itself evidence that both methods work equally well, or that the one or ones that worked well in the past will work well in the present, or that one that worked well during the ongoing normal trajectory of our present historical system would work well in the period of bifurcation and transition. What we can say is that the accumulated knowledge of world history and the vastly improved means of world communications ensure that there will be more intelligent reflection, more conscious decision making on the part of the privileged during this historical transition than during any previous one. The privileged are inevitably better informed and thereby socially smarter than they have been. They are also far wealthier, and they have far stronger and more effective means of destruction and repression than they ever did before.[11]

Wallerstein's aim isn't to frighten his readers into capitulation to the whims of the ruling class; rather he is providing a reasonable assessment of what we, mainly poor people, face as an enemy as we continue to build the type of movement necessary to win this historical battle. With more than 2 million Americans imprisoned, millions of others continually jailed and even more residing under correctional supervision and probation, more than 4 million Americans unable to participate in the electoral process because of prior felonies, one doesn't need help in comprehending which direction has been chosen by the ruling class.

To be sure, the most recent trajectory of empire signals a transition from police to prison nation-state, and those within the privileged sector have accumulated the technological weaponry necessary to wage war on the poor in this country. Some 10.6 million African Americans (1 of 4) live in poverty, thus any discussion on the repression of African Americans must be done within the context of the discourse on the war against the poor.

MUMIA ABU-JAMAL'S STORY

Mumia Abu-Jamal, it is alleged, murdered a Philadelphia policeman. This is why we are told he is on death row. However, he was targeted by the legal apparatus long before the ordeal leading to his unjust incarceration occurred. At the age of fourteen, a young Mumia was targeted for death, as were others who helped form the Philadelphia chapter of the Black Panther Party.

Having read Terry Bisson's biography, *On a Move: The Story of Mumia Abu-Jamal*,[12] and later, *We Want Freedom: A Life in the Panther Party* written by Mumia himself, I was struck by how analogous Abu-Jamal's personal narrative was to that of the broader African American experience. Bisson wrote of the changing modes of production in the South that forced millions of African Americans to migrate north in search of manufacturing jobs, reminding me of a lecture given by the eminent historian Lerone Bennett, Jr. at a meeting hosted by Catholic priest Father George Clements at his Chicago diocese during the late 1980s. Bennett spoke to a small gathering of African American clergy about this "great migration," and one of the points he made that remains fresh in my memory was the role of community in protecting and providing for orphaned children during the post-Civil War and preintegration period. Communalism was such that every child had a family, whether or not they were blood-related. Edith Cook—Abu-Jamal's mother—was one of those orphans who migrated north to Philadelphia, a city that in many ways remains more southern than most cities in the south.

Raised by his mother after his father passed, Mumia grew up in the Philadelphia projects during the waning stages of the civil rights movement, from 1954 to 1968, and like many African Americans, he has recalled not realizing he lived in poverty. But his life began as a Black Panther after being handed a copy of *The Black Panther* newspaper in the spring of 1968 by a woman named

Audrea. Soon he was frequenting Robin's bookstore in downtown Philadelphia, engaging the works of Frantz Fanon, Malcolm X, Kwame Nkrumah, Richard Wright, and Paul Robeson.

Months later, he was beaten and arrested for protesting at a rally against segregationist presidential candidate George Wallace. At fifteen he helped to organize a campaign to change his high school's name to Malcolm X High School; the same year the Federal Bureau of Investigations (FBI) began targeting him. Mumia would later join the Philadelphia Black Panther Party, eventually becoming minister of information. The FBI would eventually amass a 600-page file on his law-abiding career of helping the community; feeding breakfast to children, and selling newspapers. From his experience within the Black Panther Party, Abu-Jamal emerged as an exceptionally skilled journalist and articulate critic of empire's myriad political and social contradictions.

In his book *We Want Freedom*, Abu-Jamal laments the lack of social cohesiveness within the African American community partly brought about by new developments in information technology,

> It is striking that the present age offers scant opportunities for young rebels (and the young are ever innately rebellious!) to meet, to talk, to think, to exchange. For one thing, some bookstores, though certainly not all, are part of larger, oftentimes global, commercial networks—they are not so much meeting places as buying places.

> The internet, while pervasive in is reach, diminishes, rather than enhances social contact. One never really knows who is the recipient of a communication. Moreover, the internet is interlaced with snoops of the ubiquitous State, sniffing for any hint of rebellion as demonstrated by Project Echelon. This official paranoia is, in a sense, a reflection of a cultural change wrought by time.[13]

The comparison Mumia draws between these two social contexts within the American experience is significant. First, he is acknowledging that he came of age within the context of a social and political movement called black power. It was a time of great rebellion, as millions of people opposed the government's war in Vietnam; women, gays and lesbians, Puerto Ricans, radical whites, and Latinos began to more forcefully demand their civil rights. The year 1968 was clearly a major turning point in empire's 500-year history, and for a young person during this period, there was a social context called "the movement" shaping one's political and social consciousness. There existed a community, with institutions like bookstores, churches, and even grocery stores that cultivated a less commoditized form of human interaction. Many have confused the enhanced communications wrought by the internet with the human social contact community allows.

Today, no such social movement has been allowed to develop into a viable political and social alternative, primarily because of the lumpen-proletarization of African American youth culture, the erosion of communalism as the core ethic accompanying the African American experience, the inevitable human alienation wrought by technology in the hands of the ruling strata, and the massive imprisonment of poor people, particularly those of color and primarily African Americans. These processes eroding the communities of resistance of the 1960s were in motion during the period of Mumia's adolescence. The Black Panthers provided him an alternative.

Because of the positive impact of the Black Panther Party, a young Mumia and other youth during his time were offered a social safety net, a communal alternative to the crass consumerism and gross individualism promoted by human commoditizers propped up by capitalistic market forces in our own time. And it was a institutional weapon to fight back. Like many, Abu-Jamal survived 1968 and the tumultuous 1970s that followed. But when he was arrested in 1981, it was within what seemed to be a different political and social context altogether; that is, one outside the context of a political movement. Abu-Jamal, a hard-hitting journalist serving as president of the Association of Black Journalists in Philadelphia, was known as the "voice of the voiceless."

Determining precisely why Abu-Jamal is a political prisoner might seem, for some, conjectural at this point. Was he a victim of COINTELPRO's unfinished war against the Black Panther Party? After all, one would be both politically and historically naïve to think that the state dissolved such an entity in 1973. Or is it more likely that he was targeted because of the incisive journalism he was producing, which was exposing police brutality as well as raising the political consciousness within the African American community in Philadelphia? In fact, he was publicly warned of his penetrating and probing journalism by Philadelphia Mayor (and former police chief) Frank Rizzo. Of course, it is even more likely that it was a combination: because of his past and continued work on his community's behalf. But what the government is determined to do is the impossible, to criminalize Abu-Jamal.[14]

CONCLUSION

Abu-Jamal's case is no precedent where the issue of political imprisonment and death penalty converge. And it is not an issue limited to African American communities of resistance. In spite of a last moment stay of execution granted by Justice William O. Douglas, on June 19, 1953, Ethel and Julius Rosenberg were executed. They were tried for espionage even though the major evidence was furnished by individuals who admitted to being spies, were in prison, or already under indictment. Their case had received unprecedented worldwide support. Scientist Albert Einstein and French philosopher Jean-Paul Sartre, among many other prominent figures, had made appeals for the husband and wife. However, Supreme Court Chief Justice Frederick Vinson dispatched jets to the various places around the country where the other justices were vacationing and, together, those justices canceled Douglas's stay. Years later, a subpoenaed FBI document showed that the judge had already promised the attorney general and other high-level officials that the Rosenbergs would be executed. This was an important case because it set the tone for what would happen to those whom the government would deem "traitors" or "threats to internal security." The tragic ordeal of the Rosenbergs typified the type of naked repression that took place during the era of McCarthyism.

The 1960s marked not only a new era for an awakening blackness, but an age of increased covert government repression, surveillance, and assassinations. As the civil rights movement gave way to the black power and black liberation movements, the FBI, under the leadership of J. Edgar Hoover, intensified the war against Africans in America, radicalizing whites and indigenous peoples. Open warfare was declared against organizations such as the Black Panthers, American Indian Movement, and hundreds of others—including writers, artists, and musicians.

For African Americans, here is where the term "prisoners of war" in the United States becomes even clearer in today's context. Those who organized to defend the community's interest or spoke out against the repression were killed in assassination plots, neutralized, or were labeled criminal, convicted, and imprisoned. The counterintelligence activities carried out by the FBI was an act of war against radical, reformist, and even integrationist organizations; it was, at minimum, state-sanctioned terrorism against the general African American community.

COINTELPRO, a program that should be considered as one of many components of a wide-ranging policy of repression against African people or any individual or group who effectively opposed to its policies, was publicly exposed in 1973 after several lawsuits forced the government to release documents highlighting its various campaigns to undermine and disrupt organizations organizations deemed subversive. The public learned of how COINTELPRO contributed to the elimination and liquidation of black radical leadership and consequently the underdevelopment of the black community. But as McIntyre's *Criminalizing A Race* argues, such repression was established during the inception of the criminal justice system;[15] and as Jonathan Jackson further notes, this pattern of repression continued well into the twentieth century. In his foreword to *Soledad Brother*, Jackson makes the following observation: "COINTELPRO...was really a symptomatic, expendable entity; a small police force within a larger one (FBI), within a branch of government (executive) within the government itself (liberal democracy), within the economic system (capitalism)." Jackson goes on to point out that "doing away with COINTELPRO or even the FBI would not alter the structure that produces the surveillance/elimination apparatus."[16] This is an important observation because as the struggle around political prisoners, abolishment of the death penalty, and freedom for prisoners of war builds momentum, as well as other movements for social, political, and economic change, an incorrect analysis of what we're up against will prove more detrimental than ever, particularly given the new and more entrenched association between the social, political, and economic situation and today's new prison industry.

An unbalanced attention toward the draw-blood policies of COINTELPRO focuses in on merely one aspect of political imprisonment and repression. Mumia Abu-Jamal, for example, is one of a small number of widely recognized black "political prisoners" on death row today. However, as we continue to fight against the imminent threat of his death, there is a strong need to focus on the whole spectrum of political imprisonment, and beyond that, the entire spectrum of this economic, social, and political system.

Draconian policies toward the African American community have always created conditions that give birth to various forms of resistance. The twenty first century will be no different. The contradictions of the crime bill continue to fundamentally enhance the political, economic, and racial injustices carried out against poor white, Chicano, and African American youth within the confines of American empire. Attorney Michael Warren said in an interview in 1996, "The fact is that in a post-labor era, where people of color have not been trained for the type of technological positions in the current and emerging work force, there will be a surplus of people who are idle, and by virtue of being idle they will think about the conditions around them and will engage in activities to alleviate those conditions."[17] His remarks were instructive then, but are even more poignant at present, as unemployment among African American men in urban cities like New York City has reached over 50 percent.

It is questionable whether the present generation of young people has demonstrated the kind of political centeredness we witnessed in the 1960s and 1970s. Although today's youth embody the spirit of rebelliousness we witnessed with Fred Hampton, Sr., Assata Shakur (currently exiled in Cuba), H. Rap Brown (Imam Jamil Abdullah Al-Amin, currently imprisoned in Atlanta, Georgia), the late Kwame Ture (Stokely Carmichael was exiled in West Africa), and countless others, it is a rebelliousness that has been slow to express itself in political form.

In the present social and political context, there will be fewer youths going to prison for what appear to be political reasons. Nevertheless, with hundreds of new crime laws precisely targeted at them, the fast-paced privatization of prisons, and the hyper-marketing of the image of black youth as criminal, increasingly there will be prisoners who will, in fact, become politicized and radicalized while already incarcerated.

The conservative and reactionary antiblack rhetoric of the 1990s wasn't at all new. Code words and phrases like "war on crime" ("crime" meaning black Youth), and "The Crisis of Public Order" (the title of an *Atlantic Monthly* cover story by Adam Walinsky) were quite common in the seventeenth, eighteenth, and nineteenth centuries. Walinsky went as far as to warn his readers, "We have fled our cities. We have permitted the spread of wastelands ruled by merciless killers. We have abandoned millions of our fellow citizens to every kind of danger and degraded assault. And now a demographic surge is about to make everything worse."[18] "Stranger Murders" (murders that no longer take place among family members, or acquaintances but from violent teens)? Indeed, such rhetoric helped to reinforce a popular anti-black imagery that often reversed realities, yet it was not at all new.

If left to the dictates of the ruling class or its compliant class of political functionaries, the death penalty will not likely to be overturned anytime soon. Bill Clinton's crime bill enacted more than sixty new death penalty provisions—new federal laws that override some states that have no capital punishment. And through George W. Bush's Patriot Act, several newer death penalty provisions have been enacted, including those that would allow the state to seek the death penalty for most any form of participation in civil disobedience defined as terrorism and resulting in the death of an individual. But if, as we are often reminded, we share a responsibility in determining the fate of the world, we should immediately begin the process of refashioning the current fascist ideas governing the course of American empire.

Increasingly, African American youth will be politicized while imprisoned, and their political awakening will occur within states of confinement. One of the most well-known imprisoned political prisoners of war was George Jackson who in 1959 was sentenced to prison as a petty criminal. He was given a one-year-to-life sentence for a $70 robbery in California. However, as George Jackson became politicized, he gradually became an effective spokesperson against harsh and unfair prison conditions, and eventually emerged as one of the great revolutionary thinkers of the twentieth century. By the time his book, *Soledad Brother: The Prison Letters of George Jackson,* was published in 1969, he was one of the most recognized political prisoners in America. Less than a year after the book's publication, he was assassinated while still in prison.

Shaka Sankofa (formerly known as Gary Graham) was an angry seventeen-year-old youth when he was accused of the murder of fifty-one-year-old Bobby Grant Lambert in 1981 (see the end of Chapter 1 in this book). Sankofa roughly matched the description of Mr. Lambert's assailant in that he was a young black male. Although Sankofa admitted to carrying out several crimes during the period of his arrest, he maintained his innocence in regard to the murder of Lambert, and legal work on his behalf showed that there was overwhelming evidence to support his innocence. As he pointed out to me in an interview I conducted with him in 1996, "The criminal justice system tends to focus more sharply on the young black teenager, particularly males. It acts as a reflection of the larger society's racial prejudices and fears." Such awareness came about during the time of his imprisonment.

Sankofa would eventually emerge as a politicized anti-death penalty advocate, and because of local, national, and international support, he survived five stays of executions. The nature of his imprisonment became highly political, but as he noted, he became a political prisoner not because of any political decisions on his part that led to his incarceration, but the political decisions of others that led to his incarceration. Congress's decision, for example, to sentence crack-cocaine offenders (mostly poor persons) to five years imprisonment for procession of five grams of crack-cocaine versus the same amount of time for possessing 500 grams of cocaine, exemplifies the race and class bias among political decision-makers.

More important Sankofa became increasingly aware of the class and racial contradictions in the Texas clemency process and became an articulate opponent of it; and by inspiring prisoners around him to fight against the injustices of the death penalty, he also inspired a movement outside the prison walls. The radical ideas emanating from his political activities filtered into the streets; from Fifth Ward Houston to Brixton, United Kingdom. He envisioned the founding of a political party called Stride Toward Freedom Party that would help channel the cultural and material resources of the young hip-hop generation into a radical force within the core of American empire.

A student of history, Sankofa subscribed to principles espoused by the late revolutionary Malcolm X, most notably the right to self-defense, thus when he was given a date of execution on January 11, 1999, he called on his supporters to come to Huntsville, Texas, and defend themselves by any means necessary. "I'm not going to walk out of my cell voluntarily," he said in a press conference he called, "Nor will I allow anybody to murder me in an execution chamber without a fight. I'm prepared to die for what I believe." Sankofa was determined to die fighting, and he did.

If we continue down the road as we have, many more of the young people of today's generation may soon be faced with long prison terms and perhaps even government-sanctioned executions. Laws have already been enacted to allow the state such powers, and in view of the present conditions against the brief backdrop of history I have just discussed, Mumia Abu-Jamal represents what will happen to black people in general, but specifically to those who take on the moral and political obligation of offering their services in a vanguard capacity in the struggle to change the existing conditions African Americans face. Without an organized political body to channel such everyday forms of resistance, it might become increasingly more difficult to discern the political nature of crime.

What will become of those African Americans—those who perhaps might not have read Fanon's *Wretched of the Earth*[19]— who rebel against the increased antiblack repression? What will become of the individual who is targeted by the government henchmen simply because of the color of his skin, or the place of her origin? We already know of the existing racial inequalities within the criminal justice system, it is now time to reconstruct a new language to define the historical and politicized nature of antiblack repression and incarceration.

We are in urgent need of a victory for Mumia Abu-Jamal, because a victory for him, as well as for those countless others who remain unjustly incarcerated in empire's penal system, will be a decisive battle victory in the battle of our lives.

Afterword

In the end, the loss of empire will have less to do with constructing a counternarrative to the present master narrative than to the critical and committed engagement of all people of good will. Given the current state of Left affairs, the fact that people, not ideas alone, ultimately determine history, gives me much reason to continue hoping. That is, I have come to the conclusion that while ideas are certainly helpful in compelling people to action, it is ultimately organized action itself that will prove most decisive in ushering in the age of peace, the beloved community, the land of freedom and democracy. In this regard, I see progress being made.

I know I found hope and inspiration in the life of Shaka Sankofa, who from the dungeon of racial empire (Texas death row) transformed himself into a revolutionary leader, essentially becoming the leitmotif of a movement—a multiracial movement, in fact—that sent notice to the new emperor, then governor of Texas, George W. Bush on the eve his political coup-d'etat. Seconds before brother Sankofa was murdered, he managed to say a few last words:

> Know that I love all of you. I love the people, I love all of you for your blessing, strength, for your courage, for your dignity, the way you have come here tonight, and the way you have protested and kept this nation together. Keep moving forward, my brothers. Slavery couldn't stop us. The lynching couldn't stop us in the south. This lynching will not stop us tonight. We will go forward. Our destiny in this country is freedom and liberation. We will gain our freedom and liberation by any means necessary. . . . Keep

marching black people. Keep marching black people. They
are killing me tonight. They are murdering me tonight.[1]

Sankofa's self-transformation symbolizes the possibilities of individuals transcending their conditions and developing a political
self-consciousness. He entered the Texas prison system as an
illiterate youth but through help and self-initiative he became a
radical citizen statesman. The Cuban president Fidel Castro said
of Sankofa,

> The admirable thing about that young man, poor, mar-
> ginalized and black, and perhaps for those reasons con-
> demned to death without proof, is how during his inter-
> minable wait on death row he developed an impressive
> political and social conscience which was expressed at the
> moment of his execution. He didn't go like a lamb to the
> slaughter. He forcibly resisted the execution process right
> up until his death, as he had promised. He spoke like a
> prophet. He called for the fight to go on against what he
> called the Holocaust or Genocide that is being suffered by
> African-Americans. He demanded the vindication of his
> innocence. He died like a hero.[2]

There is inspiration in the words of the old Irish immigrant, Mary
Harris Jones, who in her late fifties embarked on a path of radical
politics that would inspire millions: "Pray for the dead and fight
like hell for the living," she was known to say. Her life is a testa-
ment to the reality that our lives are not fixed, that we know not
the hour when we're called to take action but once we embark
on the journey, never turn back, never dither. I am inspired by
the noteworthy example set forth at the First Intercontinental
Encounter for Humanity Against Neoliberalism in La Realidad
in Chiapas, Mexico, in 1996. In his closing remarks to the partici-
pants from five continents, Subcommandante Insurgente Marcos
pointed out that "In the countrysides and cities, in the states, in
the nations, on the continents, the rebels begin to recognize each
other, to know themselves as equals and different. They continue
on their fatiguing walk, walking as it is now necessary to walk,
that is to say, struggling."[3] For those who live and continue the

walk today in the urban cities of racial empire, its Appalachia Mountains, and racist rural South, the ghetto North, along the maquiladora border regions; in Cuba, Venezuela, the Mexican State of Chiapas, Columbia; and those communities of resistance throughout Africa, Asia, Eastern Europe and the Middle East, always remember the words of Bob Marley, "Emancipate yourselves from mental slavery; None but ourselves can free our minds. Have no fear for atomic energy, 'cause none of them can stop the time."

Notes

Preface

1. Houston A. Baker, Jr. *Turning South Again: Re-thinking Modernism/Re-Reading Booker T.* (Durham, NC: Duke University Press, 2001)

2. Joy James, ed., *States Of Confinement: Policing, Detentions, and Prisons* (New York: Palgrave MacMillan, 2000).

3. There is at least one significant critique of Harold Cruse that I would suggest reading. Historian Winston James's aversion to *The Crisis of the Negro Intellectual: From Its Origins To The Present* (New York: Quill, 1967) revolves primarily around Cruse's misdiagnosis of the Caribbean intellectuals, which suggested they were "conservatives fashioned in the British mold." James's book, *Holding Aloft the Banner of Ethiopia: Caribbean Radicalism in Early Twentieth-Century America* (New York: Verso, 1998) sufficiently answers many of the contradictions in Cruse's argument. However, to minimize Cruse's assertion that African Americans have been misled by "integrationists" would be a grave mistake. In addition, I also write under the assumption that other ethnic groups in America not only generally act as a nation within a nation but, with the exception of African Americans, are generally allowed to act accordingly.

4. Scott McLemee, *C.L.R. James on the "Negro Question"* (Jackson: University Press of Mississippi, 1996), p. 126.

5. William S. McFeeley, *Frederick Douglass* (New York: W.W. Norton & Company, 1991).

6. Robert C. Smith, *We Have No Leaders: African Americans in the Post-Civil Rights Era,* Forward by Ronald W. Walters (Albany: State University Press of New York, 1996), p. 280.

7.   S.E. Anderson and Tony Medina, *In Defense of Mumia: An Anthology of Prose, Poetry, and Art* (New York: Writers and Readers, 1996).

Chapter One – Rethinking Fred Gildersleeve's Lynching Photography in the Age of Legalized Lynching

1.   Washington's lynching, which took place in Waco, Texas, on May 16, 1916, became known as the "Waco Horror." The gelatin silver print was made into a real photo postcard and today provides the endpapers for Allen's book *Without Sanctuary: Lynching Photography in America (Santa Fe, NM: Twin Palm's Publishers, 2000),* which features nearly one hundred photos of lynching victims.

2.   Allen, *Without Sanctuary,* plate 23.

3.   Mary Jane Brown, *Eradicating This Evil: Women in the American Anti-lynching Movement, 1892-1940* (New York: Garland Publishing, Inc., 2000), p. 4.

4.   Ida B. Wells-Barnett, *On Lynching,* with an introduction by Patricia Hill Collins (Amherst, NY: Humanity Books, 2002), p. 147.

5.   William S. McFeely, *Frederick Douglass* (New York: W.W. Norton & Company, 1991), p. 361.

6.   Linda O. McMurry, *To Keep the Waters Troubled: The Life of Ida B. Wells* (New York: Oxford University Press, 1998), pp. 253-256.

7.   Houston A. Baker, Jr., *Turning South Again: Re-thinking Modernism/Re-Reading Booker T.* (Durham, NC: Duke University Press, 2001), p. 64.

8.   Hardly ever did an individual survive a lynching. However, James Cameron, author of the book *A Time of Terror: A Survivor's Story (Baltimore: Black Classic Press, 1994),* was a rare exception. The 1930 photo of brothers Thomas and Abram Shipp hanging from a tree in Marion, Indiana, has been widely viewed. Cameron, a sixteen-year-old, was to be the third victim, but, with the noose around his neck and the mob even more bloodthirsty after having lynched the others, he was somehow spared. Cameron describes the events leading to the lynching and his survival in the book.

9.   Howard Thurman, *The Luminous Darkness* (Richmond, IN: Friends United Press, 1989), pp. 22-23.

10. See Patricia Bernstein, *The First Waco Horror: The Lynching of Jesse Washington and the Rise of the NAACP* (College Station: Texas A&M Press, 2005), pp. 146-147.

11. W.E.B. DuBois, "The Waco Horror," *Crisis*, supplement to July 1916, p. 3.

12. Ibid., p. 2.

13. David Levering Lewis, *W.E.B. DuBois: Biography Of A Race 1868-1919* (New York: Henry Holt & Company, 1993), p. 514.

14. Patricia Bernstein, *The First Waco Horror,* pp. 89-98.

15. Jeffrey B. Perry, ed. *A Hubert Harrison Reader: Edited with Introduction and Notes* (Middletown, CT: Wesleyan University Press, 2001), p. 96.

16. Harry Haywood, *Black Bolshevik: An Autobiography of an Afro-American Communist* (Chicago: Liberator Press, 1978), pp. 49-51.

17. Brian Greer, "A Reign of Terror," *Arkansas Times*, August 4, 2000, pp. 12-19.

18. Philip Dray, *At the Hands of Person's Unknown: The Lynching of Black America* (New York: Random House, 2002), p. 146.

19. Derrick Bell, *Race, Racism and American Law, 3rd ed.* (New York: Aspen Publishers, Inc., 1992), pp. 288-289.

20. For example, numerous families were broken up because of fear of lynching. Forced migrations contributed to the economic decline of African American communities, and to the disruption of strong cultural patterns associated with their mostly agrarian lifestyles.

21. Berlin, Ira. *Many Thousands Gone: The First to Centuries of Slavery in North America.* (Cambridge, MA: The Belknap Press of Harvard University Press, 1998), pp. 4.

22. James W. Marquart, Sheldon Ekland-Olson, and Jonathan R. Sorensen, *The Rope, the Chair, & the Needle: Capital Punishment in Texas, 1923-1990* (Austin: University of Texas Press, 1998), pp. 15-16.

23. David M. Oshinsky, *"Worse than Slavery": Parchman Farm and the Ordeal of Jim Crow Justice* (New York: The Free Press, 1996), pp. 208-217.

24. Mary Frances Berry, *Black Resistance, White Law: A History of Constitutional Racism in America* (New York: Penguin Books, 1994).

25. John Eagerton, *Speak Now Against the Day: The Generation Before the Civil Rights Movement in the South* (Chapel Hill: University of North Carolina Press, 1994), pp. 123-124.

26. Harold P. Brown is credited with inventing the electric chair in 1889. He first conducted cruel experiments on animals to test the deadly effectiveness of AC voltage, and on January 1, the first electrocution law was signed into law in New York.

27. Marquart, Ekland-Olson, and Sorensen, *The Rope, The Chair, & The Needle*, p. 13.

28. Ibid, p. 18.

29. William Ecenbarger, "Perfecting Death: When The State Kills It Must Do So Humanely. Is That Possible?," *The Philadelphia Inquirer Magazine*, January 23, 1994.

30. See W. Fitzhugh Brundage, *Lynching in the New South: Georgia and Virginia, 1880-1930* (Champaign: University of Illinois Press, 1993).

31. Lou Ella Moseley, *Pioneer Days of Tyler County*, 2nd ed. (Bevil Oaks, TX: Tyler County Heritage Society, Inc., 1989), pp. 107-109.

32. William S. McFeely, "A Legacy of Slavery and Lynching: The Death Penalty As a Tool of Social Control." *The Champion Magazine Online*, Internet, November 2003, Available at http://www.criminaljustice.org/CHAMPION/ARTICLES/97nov3.htm.

33. Winthrop D. Jordon, *White Over Black: American Attitudes Toward the Negro, 1550-1812* (Chapel Hill: University of North Carolina Press, 1968), p. 121.

34. John Hope Franklin and Loren Schweninger, *Runaway Slaves: Rebels on the Plantation* (New York: Oxford University Press, 1999), p. 16.

35. Peter Irons, *A People's History of the Supreme Court* (New York: Viking Press, 1999), p. 15.

36. Sharon Patricia Holland, *Raising the Dead: Readings of Death and (Black) Subjectivity* (Durham, NC: Duke University Press, 2000), p. 14.

37. A useful analysis here would be Herbert Aptheker's chapter, "The Machinery of Control." In this book about African American rebellions against slavery, Aptheker examines the various ways in which the slave masters divided and conquered the enslaved Afri-

cans. "The fostering of division among the slaves—the ancient divide and rule formula—was an important method of control." Herbert Aptheker, *American Negro Slave Revolts, 6th ed.* (New York: International Publishers, 1993), pp. 53-78.

38. According to Alan Berlow, during George W. Bush's three terms as governor of Texas 150 men and women were executed, but many were executed based on "only the most cursory briefings on the issues in dispute. In fact, in these documents, Bush's legal counsel, Alberto R. Gonzales, repeatedly failed to apprise the governor of crucial issues in the cases at hand: ineffective counsel, conflict of interest, mitigating evidence, even actual evidence of innocence." See Alan Berlow, "The Texas Clemency Memos," *Atlantic Monthly* 292, 1 (July 29, 2003): 91.

39. See David Dow, *Executed on a Technicality: Lethal Injustice on America's Death Row* (Boston: Beacon Press, 2005), pp. 108-115.

40. Under the Texas law, this board is responsible for recommending a second reprieve to the Governor. It can also recommend the Governor commute the death sentence to a lesser sentence; recommend a reprieve and grant hearing into any part of the process; or, it can decide to not recommend commutation of the death sentence and suggest that the execution proceed, which is how the board voted, 12-5.

41. John Moritz, "Public Hearing Sought on Graham Execution," *Fort Worth Star-Telegram*, June 21, 2000, p. 1.

Chapter Two – All James T. Byrd, Jr. Wanted Was a Ride: Lynching and Police Powers in Texas

1. White supremacist John William King was convicted of James T. Byrd, Jr.'s murder and sentenced to death in February 1999; Lawrence Brewer, Jr. was convicted and sentenced to death in September 1999. Shawn Berry's trial resulted in conviction but no death penalty.

2. Amnesty International Report, *United States of America: Police Brutality and Excessive Force in New York City Police Department* (Washington, DC: AMI, 1996).

3. Human Rights Watch, *Shielded from Justice: Police Brutality and Accountability in the United States* (New York: Human Rights Watch, 1998).

4. See Peter Cassidy, "Operation Ghetto Storm: The Rise of Para-military Policing," *Covert Action Quarterly* 62 (1997): 20-25; and Reese Erlich, "Prison Labor: Workin' For the Man," *Covert Action Quarterly* 54 (1992): 58-63.

5. Ward Churchill and Jim Vander Wall, *Agents of Repression: The FBI's Secret Wars Against the Black Panther Party and the American Indian Movement* (Boston, MA: South End Press, 2002); Kenneth O'Reilly, *Racial Matters: The FBI's Secret File Black America, 1960-1972* (New York: Free Press, 1989).

6. W. Marvin Dulaney, *Black Police in America* (Bloomington: Indiana University Press, 1996), p. 2.

7. See W.E.B. DuBois, *Black Reconstruction in America* (New York: Harcourt, Brace, 1935); Rayford W. Logan, *The Betrayal of the Negro: From Rutherford B. Hayes to Woodrow Wilson* (New York: Collier Books, 1965); Hans L. Trefousse, *Reconstruction: America's First Effort at Racial Democracy* (Huntington, NY: Robert E. Krieger Publishing, 1979).

8. William Friedheim, *Freedom's Unfinished Revolution* (New York: The New Press, 1996), p. 281.

9. Jerome Miller, *Search and Destroy: African-American Males in the Criminal Justice System* (New York: Cambridge University Press, 1996), p. 53.

10. William Pierce, *The Turner Diaries* (Ft. Lee, NJ: Barricade Books, Inc., 1996).

11. Denise Hollinshed, "3 Allegedly Yelled Racial Epithets as Black Teen Dragged by Vehicle," *Houston Chronicle*, June 14, 1998, 17A.

12. Mary F. Berry, *Black Resistance, White Law: A History of Constitutional Racism in America* (New York: Penguin Books, 1994), p. 227.

13. Ibid., p. 243.

14. Richard C. Dieter, *The Future of the Death Penalty in the United States: A Texas-Sized Crisis* (Washington, DC: Death Penalty Information Center, 1994), pp. 4-13.

15. Sheila Jackson Lee introduced the Hate Crimes Prevention Act of 1999 (HR77), a bill to enhance federal enforcement of hate crimes. The Texas House passed a Hate Crimes Bill (H.B. 938)

named for James T. Byrd, Jr.; the bill failed in committee in the Texas Senate in 1999.

16. Richard Stewart and T.J. Milling, "Trio Charged in Jasper Slaying: Suspects Linked to Hate Groups," *Houston Chronicle*, June 10, 1998, pp. 1A:16A.

17. Richard Stewart and Steve Lash, "FBI Is Leading Investigation of Jasper Case: Local Authorities Welcome Help in Justice for Alleged Hate Crime," *Houston Chronicle*, June 12, 1998, p. 1A.

18. Stewart and Milling, "Trio Charged in Jasper Slaying," pp. 1A:16A.

19. See Cedric Robinson, *Black Movements in America* (New York: Routledge, 1997).

Chapter Three – African American Leadership Responses to the Increasing Significance of Whiteness

1. Some activists would consider Henry Highland Garnett's 1843 address to the slaves of the United States of America, in Buffalo, New York, to be equally significant. Read Earl Ofari, *Let Your Motto Be Resistance: The Life and Thought of Henry Highland Garnet* (Boston: Beacon Press, 1972), pp. 144-153. Also, according to Henry Louis Gates, *The Trials of Phillis Wheatley: America's First Black Poet and Her Encounters With the Founding Fathers* (New York: Basic/Civitas, 2003): William Hamilton, an antislavery figure of the 1820s, "in a speech in 1827, called Jefferson an ambidextrous philosopher 'who can reason contrariwise,' since he 'first tells you that all men are created equal,' and 'next proves that one class of men are not equal to another.' But in that same year, Hamilton himself exemplified a bit of this ambidexterity when, in a Fourth of July oration, he proposed that African Americans discontinue celebrating independence on that date. *Freedom's Journal*, in its July 11 and 18 issues, discusses the use of July 5, rather than the Fourth of July, as a sign of protest. Blacks such as William Wells Brown, Charles Lenox Remond, and Charlotte Forten all spoke or wrote about the ironies of celebrating the Fourth of July in a nation where slavery remained legal" (pp. 62-64).

2. For complete transcript of speech, refer to John Blassingame, ed., *The Frederick Douglass Papers, Series 1, vol 2* (New Haven, CT: Yale University Press, 1982), pp. 359-88.

3. In the movie *The Fugitive*, there is a scene where Harrison Ford is attempting to avoid the authorities in pursuit of him by blending into a St. Patrick's Day parade. In this scene, the African American Illinois State Comptroller and perennial gubernatorial candidate Roland Burris is conspicuously dressed in an Irish top hat, marching in the parade.

4. By "master Narrative" I mean a constructed knowledge of history that upholds the social, ideological, and political arrangements of domination. I'm speaking primarily of the national mythology regarding America's history, and am looking at it in terms of how it has been revised over a period of time to accommodate challenges presented by popular struggles that engage identity issues as well.

5. William S. McFeely, *Frederick Douglass* (New York: W. W. Norton & Company, 1991), p. 175.

6. Henry Mayer, *All on Fire: William Lloyd Garrison and the Abolition of Slavery* (New York: St. Martin's Press, 1998), p. 374.

7. Orlando Patterson, *Slavery and Social Death: A Comparative Study* (Cambridge, MA: Harvard University Press, 1987).

8. Robin Blackburn, *The Overthrow of Colonial Slavery, 1776-1848* (New York: Verso, 1996) pp. 7-13.

9. William L. Cleveland, *A History of the Modern Middle East* (Boulder, CO: Westview Press, 1994), pp. 57-78.

10. Boubacar Barry, *Senegambia and the Atlantic Slave Trade, African Studies Series 92* (New York: Cambridge University Press, 1998); Walter Rodney, *How Europe Underdeveloped Africa* (Washington, DC: Howard University Press, 1972).

11. Philip Curtin, *The Atlantic Slave Trade: A Census* (Madison, WI: University of Wisconsin Press, 1969).

12. Booker T. Washington, *Up from Slavery* (New York: Doubleday, 1901); John Hope Franklin and Alfred A. Moss, Jr., *From Slavery to Freedom: A History of African Americans,* 8th ed. (New York: Alfred K. Knopf, 2000).

13. Marimba Ani, *Yurugu: An African-centered Critique of European Cultural Thought and Behavior* (Trenton, NJ: Africa World Press, 1994).

14. John S. Haller, Jr., *Outcasts from Evolution: Scientific Attitudes of Racial Inferiority, 1859-1900* (Carbondale: Southern Illinois University Press, 1971).

15. Merton L. Dillon, *Slavery Attacked: Southern Slaves and Their Allies-1865* (Baton Rouge: Louisiana State University Press, 1990), pp. 28-29.

16. See Benjamin Quarles, *The Negro in the American Revolution*. New intro. by Gary Nash (Chapel Hill: University of North Carolina Press, 1996); also see Gary Nash, *Race and Revolution* (Madison, WI: Madison House Publishers, 1990).

17. James Oliver Horton and Lois E. Horton, *In Hope of Liberty: Culture, Community and Protest Among Northern Free Blacks, 1700-1860* (New York: Oxford, 1997), p. 80.

18. See Charshee C.L. McIntyre, *Criminalizing a Race: Free Blacks During Slavery* (Queens, NY: Kayode Press, 1992).

19. Colin G. Galloway, *The American Revolution in Indian Country: Crisis and Diversity in Native American Communities* (New York: Cambridge University Press, 1995), p. xv.

20. Edward Said, *Culture and Imperialism* (New York: Vintage Books, 1994), p. xiii.

21. Marcus Garvey, "African Fundamentalism," *Negro World* (New York), June 6, 1925.

22. Combining nationalism and communism, Ho Chi Minh would become the first president of North Vietnam, and in 1959 began the armed revolt against South Vietnam. According to Kwame Ture, in his autobiography *Ready for Revolution* (New York: Scribner, 2003), pp. 600-601, Ho Chi Minh had vivid memories of his visits to Harlem during the Garvey era: "That's when he told me that he'd been in Harlem during the time of the young Garvey. That he had thought Garvey to be a great man. That he'd heard Garvey speak and had even once made a modest financial contribution to the Garvey movement.... So we went on to discuss other matters, [and] then he suddenly leaned closer and asked, 'When are you African-Americans going to repatriate to Africa?'"

23. Alexander Crummell, *Destiny and Race: Selected Writings, 1840-1898*, edited by Wilson Jeremiah Moses (Amherst: University of Massachusetts Press, 1992); also see his *Classical Black Nationalism: From the American Revolution to Marcus Garvey* (New York: NYU Press, 1996); and Martin R. Delaney, *The Condition, Eleva-*

tion, Emigration and Destiny of the Colored People of the United States, reprinted (Baltimore: Black Classic Press, 1993).

24. Molefi K. Asante, *Afrocentricity* (Trenton, NJ: Africa World Press, 1988), p. 15.

25. See Kathleen Cleaver and George Katsiaficas, eds., *Liberation, Imagination, and the Black Panther Party: A New Look at The Panthers and Their Legacy* (New York: Routledge, 2001); Charles E. Jones, ed., *The Black Panther Party, Reconsidered* (Baltimore: Black Classic Press, 1998); Mumia Abu Jamal, *We Want Freedom: A Life in the Black Panther Party* (Boston: South End Press, 2004).

26. Gavin Menzies, *1421: The Year China Discovered America* (New York: William Morrow, 2003).

27. See Ivan Van Sertima, *They Came Before Columbus* (New York: Random House, 1976).

28. Michael C. Dawson, *Black Visions: The Roots of Contemporary African-American Political Ideologies* (Chicago: The University of Chicago Press, 2001), p. 30.

29. McFeely, *Frederick Douglass,* p. 330.

30. Haller, *Outcasts from Evolution.*

31. Josiah Clark Nott was a southerner who referred to himself as an expert in "niggerology," and wrote several widely circulated articles supporting slavery. Although a slaveowner himself, Nott claimed to be an emancipationist at heart, but felt that blacks wouldn't benefit from freedom. In his view Africans, although still an inferior species, had benefited from slavery. See Josiah Clark Nott and George Robins Gliddon, *Types of Mankind: Or, Ethnological Researches, Based Upon the Ancient Monuments, Paintings, Sculptures, and Crania of Races, and Upon Their Natural, Geographical, Philological, and Biblical History* (Philadelphia: J.B. Lippencott & Company, 1854). See William H. Tucker, *The Science and Politics of Racial Research* (Chicago: University of Illinois Press, 1994), pp. 21-22.

32. Richard J. Herrnstein and Charles Murray, *The Bell Curve: Intelligence and Class Structure in American Life* (New York: Free Press, 1994); Jared M. Diamond, *Guns, Germs, and Steel: The Fates of Human Societies* (New York: W.W. Norton & Co., 1997);

and Alfred Crosby, *The Measure of Reality: Quantification and Western Society, 1250-1600* (New York: Cambridge University Press, 1997).

33. By *real narrative*, I'm suggesting that there are alternatives to the "master narrative" that tend to generalize, and ignore the complexities of historical formation. Here I am writing as an African American, my identity having been shaped mainly by my experiences with racism in the Midwest and Southwest United States, my study of radical history, and my sustained social and political activism in anticapitalist struggles.

34. Chuck Collins and Felice Veskel (with United for a Fair Economy), *Economic Apartheid in America: A Primer on Economic Inequality & Insecurity* (New York: New Press, 2000), p. 45.

35. William Julius Wilson, *The Declining Significance of Race: Blacks and Changing American Institutions* (Chicago: University of Chicago Press, 1978).

36. Collins and Veskel, *Economic Apartheid*, p. 45.

37. See Sidney Fine, *Laissez Faire and the General-Welfare State: A Study of Conflict in American Thought, 1865-1901* (Ann Arbor: University of Michigan Press, 1964).

38. Peter Werbe, "When Work Disappears: An Interview with William Julius Wilson." The Peter Werbe Article Database. Online, Internet, November 17, 1997, Available at http://www.goodfelloweb.com/Werbe/Williams/htm.

39. David Wessel, "Racial Discrimination: Still At Work in the U.S." *The Wall Street Journal Online*, Internet, September 4, 2003, Available at http://www.careerjournal.com/myc/diversity/20030916-wessel.html.

40. Harry J. Holzer and Paul Offner, "The Puzzle of Black Male Unemployment," *The Public Interest* 154 (Winter 2004): 74-84

41. Cynthia Hamilton, "From Streets of Hope to Landscapes of Despair: The Case of Los Angeles," in James Jennings, ed., *Race & Politics* (New York: Verso, 1997). I am hesitant to use the word community here because it implies that blacks at some point controlled the geographical spaces in which they resided.

Hamilton's point suffices but blacks have generally lived under continual white domination since their arrival. The postslavery

conditions, though, have worsened because of massive despacial-
ization, which has made it difficult for communities of resistance
form and to sustain themselves.

42. The Democratic Leadership Conference is an organization founded
in 1985 to advocate democratic capitalism and to move the Democratic Party in a more centrist and conservative direction.

43. Robert C. Smith, *Racism in the Post-Civil Rights Era: Now You
See It, Now You Don't* (Albany: State University Press of New
York, 1995), pp. 112-139.

44. William J. Clinton, *My Life* (New York: Alfred K. Knopf, 2004),
p. 339.

45. Ronald W. Walters and Robert C. Smith, *African American Leadership* (Albany: State University Press of New York, 1999), p. 82.

46. Vernon E. Jordan, Jr. with Annette Gordon-Reed, *Vernon Can
Read!* (New York: Basic Books, 2001), pp. 232-234.

47. See Robert L. Allen, *Black Awakening in Capitalist America*
(Trenton, NJ: Africa World Press, 1990).

48. Michael Schwartz, ed. *Larry Neal, Visions of a Liberated Future:
Black Arts Movement Writings, with commentary by Amiri
Baraka, Stanley Crouch, Charles Fuller, and Jayne Cortez* (New
York: Thunder's Mouth Press, 1989) pp. 133-143.

49. Robert B. Hill, *The Illusion of Black Progress* (Washington, DC:
National Urban League Research Department, 1978).

50. Hill provides a summary of his findings as a preface to the study.
I have just provided an overview of that summary.

51. While this book doesn't focus directly on African American
leadership, for an excellent analysis of how Corporate America
responded to radicalism of the late 1960s see Allen, *Black Awakening in Capitalist America.*

52. Henry Louis Gates and Cornel West, *The Future of the Race* (New
York: Alfred K Knopf, 1996), p. 4.

53. Michael C. Dawson provides a useful examination of present-day
class tensions within the African American community, *Behind
the Mule: Race and Class in African-American Politics* (Princeton,
NJ: Princeton University Press, 1994).

54. Wilson, *Declining Significance*, p. 139.

55. For insightful analysis on urban struggle, see Stephen Nathan Haynes, *Race, Culture, and the City: A Pedagogy for Black Urban Struggle* (Albany: SUNY Press, 1995).

56. Read the chapter, "Carter-Reagan-Bush: The Bipartisan Consensus" in Howard Zinn's, *A People's History of the United States 1492-Present*, rev. ed. (New York: HarperPerrenial, 1995), pp. 551-588.

57. George Winslow, *Capital Crimes* (New York: Monthly Review Press) pp. 163-167.

58. See Marc Maur (with the Sentencing Project), *Race to Incarcerate* (New York: New Press, 1999); Christian Parenti, *Lockdown America: Police and Prisons in the Age of Crisis* (New York: Verso, 1999); Gary Webb, *Dark Alliance: The CIA, The Contras, and the Crack Cocaine Explosion* (New York: Seven Stories Press, 1999).

59. Toni Cade Bambara, "The African American Writer and the Mass Media: Black Images in Print Media" (Dallas, TX: The Third Eye, 5th Annual Black Awakening Conference, November 5, 1989).

60. Nikhil Pal Singh, "Toward an Effective Antiracism," in Manning Marable, ed., *Dispatches from the Ebony Tower* (New York: Columbia University Press, 2000), pp. 32-33.

61. Larvester Gaither, "Race & Class: Dialogue with A. Sivanandan," *The Gaither Reporter*, vol. 2, no 8 (June 1995), pp. 1-6.

62. Manning Marable, *Talking About a Revolution* (Boston: South End Press, 1998), p. 92.

63. Manning Marable, *Beyond Black and White: Rethinking Race in American Politics and Society* (New York: Verso, 1996) p. 159.

64. Ibid., p. 161.

65. Cornel West, ed., *The Cornel West Reader* (New York: Basic/ Civitis Books, 1999), p. 524.

66. Cornel West, *The Cornel West Reader*, p. 524.

67. George Yancy, ed., *Cornel West: A Critical Reader* (Malden, MA: Blackwell, 2001) p. 358.

68. Jeffrey B. Perry, ed., *A Hubert Harrison Reader, Edited with Introduction and Notes* (Middletown, CT: Wesleyan University Press, 2000), p. 4.

69. C.L.R. James, "Nkrumah, Padmore, and the Ghanian Revolution," (Washington, D.C: Institute of the Black World, June 17, 1971).

70. George Padmore, *How Britain Rules Africa* (New York: Negro Universities Press, 1969); Padmore, *Pan Africanism or Communism*, Foreword by Richard Wright. Introduction by Azinna Nwafor (Garden City, NY: Doubleday, 1971).

71. Ibid. James, "Nkrumah, Padmore, and the Ghanian Revolution."

72. Gates and West, *The Future of the Race*, pp. 36-37.

73. Identity movement is usually derogatively defined by Leftist terms, but I'm referring to movements that place importance on distinguishing their more immediate issues from the broader issues around them. It doesn't necessarily mean they ignore the broader issues; in fact, more often than not the immediate and broader issues will coalesce at some point in the struggle.

74. Lothrop Stoddard, *The Rising Tide of Color Against White World-Supremacy*. With Introduction by Madison Grant (New York: Scribner, 1920).

75. Madison Grant, *The Passing of A Great Race; The Racial Basis of European History*, 4th ed. With a documentary supplement (New York: Scribner's Sons, 1921).

76. Jared Taylor is a self-described race relations expert. He publishes *American Renaissance*, which promotes pseudoscientific studies about race and culture in America. See Jared Taylor, *Paved With Good Intentions: The Failure of Race Relations in Contemporary America* (New York: Carol & Graf Publishers, Inc., 1992). University of Western Ontario professor Phillippe Rushton lectures on ethnic variations and evolutionary psychology. He has suggested that African Americans possess smaller brains than their American counterparts.

77. James Baldwin, *The Fire Next Time* (New York: Vintage Press International Edition, 1993), p. 104.

78. George Yancey, *Who Is White? Latinos, Asians, and the New Black/Nonblack Divide* (Boulder, CO: Lynne Rienner, 2003).

79. Arthur M. Schlesinger, *The Disuniting of America* (New York: W.W. Norton & Company, 1992).

80. Schlesinger is quoting from a book written by Frenchman Hector St. John de Crèvecoeur in the mid-eighteenth century, *Letters from an American Farmer*. "He is an American, who leaving behind him all his ancient prejudices and manners, receives new

ones from the new mode of life he has embraced, the new govern-ment he obeys, and the new rank he holds. The American is a new man, who acts upon new principles.... Here individuals of all nations are melted into a new race of men."

81. Ibid., p.15.

82. Ibid., p. 14.

83. Ibid., p. 92.

84. Molefi K. Asante, *Malcolm X as Cultural Hero & Other Afrocen-tric Essays* (Trenton, NJ: Africa World Press, 1993), p.85.

85. Michael Angelo Gomez, *Exchanging Our Country Marks: The Transformation of African Identities in the Colonial and Antebel-lum South* (Chapel Hill: University of North Carolina Press, 1998); Peter Wood, *Black Majority: Negroes in Colonial South Carolina from 1670 through the Stono Rebellion* (New York: Norton, 1975).

86. Colin A. Palmer, *Passageways: An Interpretive History of Black America. Volume I: 1619-1863* (Orlando, FL: Holt, Rinehart and Winston, 1998), p. 27.

87. Joseph E. Inikori and Stanley L. Engerman, eds., *The Atlantic Slave Trade: Effects on Economics, Societies, and Peoples in Africa, the Americas, and Europe* (Durham, NC: Duke University Press, 1992), p. 9.

88. The model minority thesis has been in currency for more than four decades, coined by sociologist William Peterson, who con-cluded that Japanese Americans owed their success in "overcom-ing prejudice" to culture, strong work ethic, and family values. The argument has been used to further stereotype African Ameri-cans who remain economically disadvantaged.

89. Walter Williams, *The State Against Blacks* (New York: McGraw-Hill Book Company, 1982), p. xvi.

90. Howard Kurtz, "Administration Paid Commentator: Education Department Used Williams To Promote "No Child" Law," *Wash-ington Post*, January 8, 2005, p. A01.

91. In this particular chapter, I do not discuss the failure of post-civil rights leadership. By and large, it is an accommodationist class that plays a role similar to the *comprador* classes in Central and South America, the royal families in the Arab world, and others. In

examining black struggle, one cannot make the mistake of relying on the media to identify political, cultural, and social trends. For example, Reverend Jesse Jackson has amassed a personal fortune by undermining various protest initiatives. Thus, Walter Williams's critique might appear useful to one whose social and political awareness is informed by the mainstream media.

92. For Walter Williams's analysis of reparations, read, Walter Williams, "Reparations for Slavery." *Capitalism Magazine*, Online, Internet, January 12, 2001, Available WWW: http://www.capmag.com/article.asp?ID=89.

93. John Higham, *Strangers in the Land: Patterns of American Nativism, 1860-1925,* 2nd ed. (New Brunswick, NJ: Rutgers University Press, 1988).

94. Betty Wood, *The Origins of American Slavery: Freedom and Bondage in the English Colonies* (New York: Hill & Wang, 1997).

95. See Theodore W. Allen, *The Invention of the White Race: Racial Oppression and Social Control,* Vol. 1 (New York: Verso Press, 1994), and his *The Invention of the White Race: The Origin of Racial Oppression in Anglo-America,* Vol. II (New York: Verso Press, 1997); and David R. Roediger, *The Wages of Whiteness: Race and the Making of the American Working Class,* rev. ed. (New York: Verso Press, 1999).

96. Generally speaking, few African Americans advocate amalgamation publicly. There are some exceptions, however. See John H. McWhorter, *Losing the Race: Self-Sabotage in Black America* (New York: The Free Press), p. 258.

97. Anna Grimshaw, ed., *The C.L.R. James Reader* (Oxford, UK: Blackwell, 1992), p. 402.

98. David Levering Lewis, *W.E.B. DuBois: Biography of a Race 1868-1919* (New York: Henry Holt and Company, 1993), pp. 555-580.

99. Grimshaw, *The C.L.R. James Reader,* pp. 402-403.

100. See Peter Linebaugh and Marcus Rediker, *The Many-Headed Hydra: Sailors, Slaves, Commoners, and the Hidden History of the Revolutionary Atlantic* (Boston: Beacon Press, 2001).

101. Anne D. Neal and Jerry L. Martin, Defending Civilization: How Our Universities Are Failing America and What Can Be Done

About It (Washington, DC: American Council of Trustees and Alumni, 2001).

102. David Allan Bloom, *The Closing of the American Mind* (New York: Simon & Schuster, 1988).

103. Neal and Martin, *Defending Civilization*, pp. 6-7.

104. Roberto J. Gonzalez, "Lynne Cheney-Joe Lieberman Group Puts Out a Blacklist," *San Jose Mercury News*, December 13, 2001

105. Neal and Martin, *Defending Civilization*, p. 6.

106. See Marable, *Beyond Black and White;* also see Stephen Howe, *Afrocentrism: Mythical Pasts and Imagined Homes* (New York: Verso Press, 1998).

107. William Julius Wilson, *The Bridge Over The Racial Divide: Rising Inequality and Coalition Politics* (Berkeley: University of California Press, 1999).

108. Roberto Unger and Cornel West, *The Future of American Progressivism: An Initiative For Political and Economic Reform* (Boston, MA: Beacon Press, 1998).

109. Struve argued for a gradual transition from capitalism to socialism through various liberal reforms, and possessed little faith in the capacity of the proletariat, insisting that they must be aided and guided by the liberal bourgeoisie.

110. Immanuel Wallerstein, *Utopistics: Or, Historical Choices of the Twenty-first Century* (New York: The New Press, 1998).

Chapter Four – Black Movements Toward Freedom: Mumia Abu-Jamal and Empire's Prisoners of War

1.   Mumia Abu-Jamal: *We Want Freedom: A Life in the Panther Party,* with introduction by Kathleen Cleaver (Boston: South End Press, 2004); *Death Blossoms: Reflections from a Prisoner of Conscience* (Farmington, PA: The Plough Publishing House, 1997); *All Things Censored* (New York: Seven Stories Press, 2000); *Live From Death Row* (New York: Addison-Wesley Publishing House, 1995); *Our Fathers: An Examination of the Spiritual Life of African and African American People* (Trenton, NJ: Africa World Press, 2003).

2.   Dana Priest, "CIA Holds Terror Suspects in Secret Prisons," *The Washington Post*, November 2, 2005, p. A01.

3.   Luis P. Carilles is accused of sabotaging a Cuban airliner in 1976 that killed 73 people. Some U.S. political leaders have attempted to forestall his extradition and offer political asylum, citing the political asylum offered to Assata Shakur by the Cuban government.

4.   Larvester Gaither, "Conviction Or A Fine?: Are There Political Prisoners and POWs in the Good Ole US of A?," S.E. Anderson and Tony Medina, eds. *In Defense of Mumia: An Anthology of Prose, Poetry, and Art* (New York: Writers and Readers, 1996), p. 146.

5.   James Oliver Horton, and Lois E. Horton, *In Hope of Liberty: Culture, Community and Protest Among Northern Free Blacks, 1700-1860* (New York: Oxford University Press, 1997), p. 62.

6.   Frederic Bancroft, *Slave Trading in the Old South*, with new intro. by Michael Tadman (Columbia: University of South Carolina Press, 1996), pp. 17-18.

7.   Charshee Lawrence McIntyre, *Criminalizing a Race* (Queens, NY: Kayode Press, 1992), p. ix.

8.   Paul Finkelman, *Dred Scott v. Sandford: A Brief History with Documents* (New York: Bedford Books, 1997).

9.   Scott McLemee, ed., *C.L.R. James on the "Negro Question"* (Jackson: University Press of Mississippi, 1996) pp. 94-95.

10. See Stetson Kennedy, *After Appomattox: How the South Won the War* (Miami: University Press of Florida, 1995).

11. Immanuel Wallerstein, *Utopistics: Or, Historical Choices of the Twenty-first Century* (New York: New Press, 1998) pp. 82-83.

12. Terry Bisson, *On A Move: The Story of Mumia Abu-Jamal* (Plough Publishing House, 2001).

13. Abu-Jamal, *We Want Freedom*, p. 248.

14. See James Owens, "Mumia Abu-Jamal: The ABC Hatchet Job" *Covert Action Quarterly*, No. 67, Spring/Summer 1999: 37-47.

15. McIntyre, *Criminalizing a Race*.

16. George Jackson, *Soledad Brother: The Prison Letters of George Jackson* (Chicago: Lawrence Hill Books, 1994), pp. xiii-xxv.

17. Larvester Gaither, "Are There Any Political Prisoners," p. 148.

18. Adam Walinsky, "The Crisis of Public Order," *The Atlantic Monthly*, July 1995, pp. 39-54.

19. Frantz Fanon, *Wretched of the Earth*, Preface by Jean-Paul Sartre (New York: Grove Press, 1963).

Afterword

1. Gary Graham, "Last Statement," *Texas Department of Criminal Justice: Executed Offenders*. Online, Internet, June 22, 2000, Available at http://www.tdcj.state.tx.us/stat/executed offenders.htm.

2. Fidel Castro, "Tribute to Shaka Sankofa." *GRANMA*. Online, Internet, June 24, 2000, Available at http://www.granma.cu/ingles/june4/27version-i.html.

3. Greg Ruggiero and Stuart Sahulka, eds., *Zapatista Encuentro: Documents from the 1996 Encounter for Humanity Against Neoliberalism*, The Open Media Pamphlet Series (New York: Seven Stories Press, 1996), pp. 31-58.

Index